The Silence of God

Selections from *A Film Trilogy* by Ingmar Bergman copyright
© 1967 by Calder and Boyars. Reprinted by permission of
Grossman Publishers, Inc. and Calder and Boyars.
Selections from *Four Screen Plays* by Ingmar Bergman copyright
© 1960 by Simon & Schuster, Inc. Reprinted by permission of
Simon & Schuster, Inc. and Lorrimer Publishers.
Frame enlargements (pages 8, 16, 38, 56, 76, 96, 116, and
154) are printed with the kind permission of Janus Films
(A. William J. Becker III and Saul Turell).
Photograph from *Persona* (page 134) is printed through the
courtesy of United Artists Corporation.

LIBRARY OF CONGRESS CATALOG CARD NUMBER: 76-85048

ISBN 0-88946-951-2

CONTENTS

Pictures appear on 8, 16, 38, 56, 76, 96, 116, 134, 154.

To Iceland
The Physical Landscape
of the Silence of God

The Silence of God

The Silence

Modern atheists have often done themselves a drastic injustice by entirely neglecting one poignant psychological strand of their own atheism. Overzealous theists have often trivialized that same psychological strand or impermissibly used it to explain away atheism, to psychoanalyze it out of existence in a manner not much better or nobler than that in which certain brash modern critics psychoanalyze away mystical experience. This psychological strand of modern atheism can be articulated thus: I do not hear or see or feel or in any way experience this God whom many have claimed to experience as the lodestar of their strivings and the comfort and bulwark of their faltering efforts.

Here we are entirely arrived at the level of neat personal experience; here it is totally irrelevant and crass to come initially armed with logical arguments and still worse to interpose pretentious psychological explanations that are supposed to explain away; here, to an even greater extent than in the case of the articulation of atheistic ultimates, it is mandatory to listen sympathetically.

Fortunately this signal and stunning experience, peculiar—at least in its intensity and modality—to modern man, has been articulated in all the complexity of its tortuous dynamic by an outstanding contemporary technician of the film art. Ingmar Bergman's critics are often openly bemused at his capacity to produce film after film of stranger and stranger content, even of more and more surrealistic style, without ever slipping into unintelligibility or pompous pretentiousness. I believe a recent Bergman commentator has hit upon the deepest reason for this capacity when he writes: "Ingmar Bergman's ability to combine the greatest universality with the most delicate intimacy of situation and characterization gives his films something of the power of myth.[1]

The film art, a typically twentieth-century invention, is a recognizably unique medium, conveying its message by an orchestration of words, pictures, and music. Bergman has always, therefore, resolutely refused to "interpret" his films; he quite rightly points out that he has expended immense energy precisely on the film orchestration and consequently is persuaded the communication must rest on that orchestration. He will readily allow a multitude of divergent interpretations and steadfastly refuse to adjudicate between them. I shall here attempt one such interpretation.

Bergman points up the existential and even drastically neural dimension of the genesis of his own films:

> A film for me begins with something very vague—a chance remark or a bit of conversation, a hazy but agreeable event unrelated to any particular situation. It can be a few bars of music, a shaft of light across the street.[2]

And he pinpoints the subsequent unique operation of the film craft:

> Film has nothing to do with literature; the character and substance of the two art forms are usually in conflict. . . . When we experience a film, we consciously prime ourselves for illusion. Putting aside will and intellect, we make way for it in our imagination. The sequence of pictures plays directly on our feelings.[3]

The film sequence, the series of interconnected film articulations I shall here try to examine, is no mere neat syllogistic chain of argumentation. Bergman himself remarks: "I try to tell the truth about the human condition, the truth as I see it." [4] Yet he proceeds to insist that this description of his aims is evasive; and he describes his general purpose in his films in terms of the old story about the rebuilding of the cathedral of Chartres:

> I want to be one of the artists in the cathedral on the great plain. I want to make a dragon's head, an angel, a devil—or perhaps a saint—out of stone.[5]

Above all, Bergman wants his films to communicate. He exclaims bitterly and poignantly against the failure of communication in the heyday of modern individualism:

> It is my opinion that art lost its basic creative drive the moment it was separated from worship. . . . Today the individual has become the highest form and the greatest bane of artistic creation. The smallest wound or pain of the ego is examined under a microscope as if it were of eternal importance. The artist considers his isolation, his subjectivity, his individualism almost holy. Thus we finally gather in one large pen, where we stand and bleat about our loneliness without listening to each other and without realizing that we are smothering each other to death. The individualists stare into each other's eyes and yet deny the existence of each other.[6]

Bergman certainly did not intend his films to be received entirely passively; the sensitized utterly passive filmstrip is a mere storage and communication device. On either side of it stand human beings, calling to one another as deep to deep. This book is the answer of one such human being, preoccupied with the problem and the phenomenon of modern atheism, to that other human being who exposed on film his own inner vision.

Bergman begins with the soul of modern man, with the doubt, torment, fragile hope, excruciating anguish, of that soul. Such an approach can never produce a superficially comforting religious film. Indeed it can truly be said that as the film series proceeds, the shadows become ever darker and more menacing. The final film of the series I examine has been called a film utterly without hope, a perfect proclamation of hopeless atheism.

Such a progressively more somber interpretation seems to me entirely to disregard certain definite hints in these films. It is these hints I shall endeavor to collate and interpret into a quite different culminating picture.

I am not for an instant presuming to interpret the inner course of Bergman's personal dynamic. I am simply working with and upon what has been surrendered to us all by his films. My text, my original, is Bergman's cumulative witness throughout these seven films.

Three persistent and intensifying impressions assail me as I contemplate the consistent whole that is the film series.

1. An initial absence gradually evolves into a disturbing and terrifying presence. There gradually emerges that conviction that theists all too often flippantly cast aside in mistaken reverence or dubious pusillanimity: the ultimate religious experience— which is the only truly religious experience—is supremely personal *on both sides*: man is reacting not to a mathematical formula but to a living God, and because this living God is communicating not with a sensitized passive photographic plate but rather with the endless restlessness that is a human person, the dialogue must have the gaps and terrors incident upon all personal communication. Because the divine communicator is utterly other than his creature, the communication will often be trammeled by the limitations and always by the unstable freedom of the human partner. But *God is operative* and communicative throughout these films. Their theme is truly the silence *of* God, not merely the silence that proves there is no God there. When finally encountered head-on, this God is dramatically exposed to his own creature who can reject him.

2. Indeed the dynamic of these seven films *begins with man and ends with God.* I see that dynamic sweeping aside restrictive humanism and geometricizing transcendentalism alike. *Love* is its Alpha and Omega; but what a purifying furnace must not that love traverse between the beginning and the consummation! The trenchant thrust of human longing for certitude and

peace and hope for pain is its powering drive; tortuously and deviously that thrust reveals itself as questing, probing, evading, facing, and suffering before it is finally brought to the awful moment of vision. At the beginning, there is a silence that is held to be the proof of God's inexistence. At the end there is a still more awful silence which reveals itself as the true silence *of* God. The God imagined to be nonexistent because silent reveals his face as precisely the ultimate respecter of human freedom, whose unflinching rendezvous with man is a supremely immanent or incarnational one.

3. *Not only man but also God proceeds through a dynamic evolution* in the course of these films: from an initial serene intransigence to a terminal agonizing involvement. This is what the Incarnation is really all about. And transcendentalist Monophysitism has most brutally savaged the genuine poetic insight of Christians into the reality of this great event, which here emerges so drastically. These films, taken as an integral whole, reveal the mystery of the Incarnation in an absolutely uncompromising way. No room is left for poetic sentimentality, but no whit of ontological poignancy is lost. Moreover, God looms into these films in two ways, each with its own peculiar dynamic: first, there is the felt absence growing gradually throughout the course of the seven films into a more terribly felt presence; then there is the artistic presence of God in a series of characters who "play" God in the sense of rendering present some portion of his dynamic and problematic in his relation with his creatures. The poet can essay what the theologian must sedulously avoid, the penetration, by poetic language and plastic representation, of the dimension of mystery. If the theologian writes in this vein he lapses into unedifying and unappetizing heresy; but the poet can touch the very nerve of the living God in commerce with his living creatures and expose the stunning love affair so long raging between them. This Bergman does: the dynamic of the ontological absence-presence of God runs exactly parallel to the dynamic of the God-mouthpieces. As these mouthpieces

become more and more fleshed out, more and more adequate to the reality, so is the initial gnawing absence gradually replaced and supplanted by a terrifying and challenging presence.

But besides a supreme God-mouthpiece, each film in this series has likewise one character who is the epitome of seeking humanity (and since humanity's seeking is itself ambivalent, part real searching and part rebellious febrile fleeing, so the individual film may have more than one such epitome of humanity). And the line of the dynamic of the human seekers runs exactly counter to the line of the God-mouthpieces: as the God-mouthpieces become progressively more complex and austere, so the epitomes of human seeking becomes progressively simpler and more engaging or more reprehensible.

The radically simplified problematic of the entire series, regarded as a solidary unity, might be stated thus. The initial questioning demands: Is God *there?* And the terminal answer retorts: No, now he is *here!*

Any question of "adequacy" of this interpretation here offered to the "original" Bergman is patently irrelevant. I am neither trying to wrest Bergman to my own aims and ends nor attempting to offer an exclusive key. Rather this book is offered as a testimony to the thought patterns and above all the picture kaleidoscope activated in me by the experience of these films. This experience, over a period of seven years of seeing the films in the order in which they were produced, has led me, whom events have molded into a psychologically convinced Christian theist, through a dark valley of the anguish typical of modern man precisely as modern man is both product and producer of the twentieth century. This anguish is not to be dismissed lightly by anyone who holds that man, as free evolving creature, is being progressively loaded with more and more responsibility in the evolution and transformation (indeed transfiguration and even, if you will, transubstantiation) of the cosmos. This anguish is an integral part of the science of God, a science that is but the pale rationalized articulation of a primordial experience of which the paradigm is the burning bush that was not consumed.

THE SILENCE

The testimony that is this book is intended to complement the testimony that is *The Faith of the Atheist*. Whereas that investigation was preeminently a theo*logical* one, this is intended as a theo*aesthetic* one. It is intended furthermore as a dialogue with those modern atheists who can and do sincerely assert that God's silence is the basis of their unbelief. Or, more fairly and accurately, who say that they find only a silence where their interlocutor finds the radiant face of God and hears his mighty voice, that they do not find human existence a prelude to eternal happiness but a journey terminating in death which is the end.

Because I have wished this testimony to be preeminently an inner dialogue and testimony and not a theological exposition, I have deliberately absented myself from familiar surroundings and the pleasant clamor of accordant and dissident voices for the writing of it. I must pay my warm tribute of thanks to the northern island that has offered me hospitality that respects solitude and a landscape that is instructive without being distracting. Iceland seems to me to typify the physical counterpart of the spiritual landscape of God's silence. And if he looms majestically and awesomely present after the heart has become accustomed to the denudation of distracting frills, then that presence is not of the kind any southern seeker would have imagined as that pusillanimous voyager tried to leap the inescapable gap or circumvent the dark valley.

FORMULATING

The Seventh Seal

I call out to him in the dark but no one seems to be there.

A knight, Antonius Block, is returning from a protracted absence on a crusade. On the seacoast of his native land he encounters Death and begins playing chess with him. Their game is interrupted as Block and his squire, Jöns, ride on to new adventures, while the viewer is introduced to Jof the juggler, his wife, Mia, and their baby son. Jof sees visions, the Virgin Mary, angels, and devils. Skat, their "business manager," is practicing a part for the saints' feast in Elsinore. Jöns and Block ride up to a little gray stone church, where Block tries to ease his soul in the confessional, only to find he has been confessing to Death concealed behind the grille. Death invites him to continue their chess game later. Jöns and Block now encounter four soldiers and a monk putting a young girl, Tyan, into the stocks: she is to be burned at the stake as a witch, suspected of causing the plague that is infesting the country. Riding on, Block and

Jöns become thirsty, and the squire, looking for a well, encounters the seminarian Raval, who had persuaded Block ten years previously to go to the crusade; Raval, who has just pilfered a ring from a woman dead of the plague, is molesting a young girl. Jöns scares him off and the girl somewhat aimlessly follows Jöns. Squire, knight, and girl travel on to Embarrassment Inn, where Mia, Jof, and Skat are performing. Flagellants in procession interrupt the performance, and a monk denounces the sinful crowd, threatening them with the plague death. Jöns makes the acquaintance of Plog, a smith who is disconsolately looking for his wife, Lisa, whom he suspects of having run off with some actor. Jof likewise meets Plog and hears his tale of marital woe; Raval intervenes to taunt the little juggler Jof and set Plog against Jof by voicing the suspicion that Jof's partner may be the very actor with whom Lisa has eloped. Warming to his cruel sport, Raval makes poor Jof dance like a bear on the table, until Jöns intervenes and slashes Raval's face.

The scene moves to the juggler's wagon, where the knight is meeting Mia and the baby. Jof staggers in, badly mauled, and is ministered to by Mia. The knight joins them in a frugal meal: wild strawberries and milk. He invites the juggler and family to join the knight's party for the dangerous ride through the forest. The knight moves off to continue his chess game with Death. Soon, however, the game is again interrupted by the arriving juggler's party, now joined by old Plog; all begin to move through the forest. Soon they encounter the procession bringing the young witch to the place of burning; the knight strives in vain to comfort the poor child, who is persuaded Satan will protect her from all harm. The voyagers continue and soon chance upon Lisa, who has indeed eloped with Skat but immediately deserts him to return penitently to her husband, blaming Skat for her waywardness. Though poor Plog fulminates and seeks to goad Skat into a fight, the wily actor prefers a melodramatic fake self-stabbing scene. The party moves on through the forest, and Skat finds himself treed by Death, who is sawing down the actor's perch. Death remains impervious to all Skat's wiles. The tree falls and the forest is silent.

At dawn the travelers encounter Raval again, now mortally sick of the plague and begging for water. He dies a little distance from them, kept at arm's length for fear of infection. The knight resumes his chess game with Death, and Jof and Mia, with their baby son, slip away through a menacing storm. Death finally checkmates Block.

The knight later has brought his other companions to his castle, where his wife, Karin, is awaiting them. They break bread together while Karin reads from the Apocalypse. Soon there comes an insistent, implacable knock. Death has come.

In the light of a watery dawn, Jof and Mia have safely reached a haven of refuge. Jof sees a final vision: the entire party of their friends of the night before being conducted by Death in a solemn dance away up the hills into the dark lands. Mia affectionately reproves her husband for his too vivid imagination.

Such is the fast-moving episodic medieval mystery play Bergman presents as *The Seventh Seal*. Bergman is most keenly interested in modern man, but he never confuses the adjective with the substantive. Taking full cognizance always of the differentiating specificity of a twentieth-century human individual or group, Bergman yet endeavors to penetrate via this specificity to a perennial human reality of which the specificity is a mere modality. Thus, the film in which the entire silence-of-God problematic is formulated is set in the Middle Ages, as if deliberately to highlight the transtemporal and transsituational validity of the problematic it presents. If we discard the minor characters, who portray the usual innumerable shadings of the human estate, we easily discover the two epitomes of humanity in the knight (the tormented earnest seeker, the would-be believer) and the squire (the cynical but compassionate disbeliever in any religious reconciliation). In this first of Bergman's films directly concerned with the silence-of-God problematic, God is an enormous absence, almost palpably felt as such. Yet there is a God-mouthpiece in this film: Death himself, grim, devious, and implacable, but not without flashes of dry humor, and emerging at the end in a vision of peripheral Everyman (Jof the juggler) as austerely kind and beneficent.

The background of the drastic, simple, and radical encounter between the knight and Death is the complex anguish of a medieval community beset by the stalking horror of death in a much more hideous form, the plague. This motley community, like all human grouping everywhere, spawns a multitude of variants of its basic dread—and hope!

There are the flagellants and the doomsaying priests who lash the populace physically and verbally to penance for the sins they allege must have been responsible for this divine chastisement; and then forecast an implacable doom despite all repentance:

> God has sentenced us to punishment. We shall all perish in the black death. . . . Death stands right behind you. I can see how his crown gleams in the sun. His scythe flashes as he raises it above your heads. . . . Do you know, you insensible fools, that you shall die today or tomorrow, or the next day, because all of you have been sentenced? Do you hear what I say? Do you hear the word? You have been sentenced, sentenced! . . . Lord have mercy on us in our humiliation! Don't turn your face from us in loathing and contempt, but be merciful to us for the sake of your son, Jesus Christ.[1]

This milieu and spiritual-psychological background is evocative of Albert Camus' picture in *The Plague* of the doomed city of Oran and Father Paneloux's first fire-and-brimstone sermon. For the whole penance pericope seems pure formality, and the monk seems to take feverish delight in lacerating the populace brutally with the inevitability of a doom that the hand of man cannot prevent, for it hangs perpetually in the stagnant air that mortals breathe.

There is the pitiful young witch, Tyan, who seeks escape from the utter boredom and emptiness of everyday life in imaginative intercourse with the Devil:

> But he is with me everywhere. I only have to stretch out my hand and I can feel his hand. He is with me now too. The fire won't hurt me. He will protect me from everything evil.[2]

This poignant trust of Tyan in a transcendental diabolical power able to protect her is in sharp and relentless contrast with the knight's anguished outcry concerning his God: "I call out to him in the dark but no one seems to be there." [3] But the supreme irony is not the mere inversion of religious values implied in the supposition that the devil can protect from evil (in the sense, even, of ill or harm) but rather in the weird and awful climax of Tyan's miserable little saga, surely the supremely horrible moment of this somber and terrifying film. As the young witch is being burned at the stake, the squire reveals at once his cynicism and his compassion, his vulnerable compassion, and articulates the quintessence of the total-silence problem in this interchange with the knight:

JÖNS: What does she see? Can you tell me?
KNIGHT (*shakes his head*): She feels no more pain.
JÖNS: You don't answer my question. Who watches over that child? Is it the angels, or God, or the Devil, or only the emptiness? Emptiness, my lord!
KNIGHT: This cannot be.
JÖNS: Look at her eyes, my lord. Her poor brain has just made a discovery. Emptiness under the moon.
KNIGHT: No.
JÖNS: We stand powerless, our arms hanging at our sides, because we see what she sees, and our terror and hers are the same. (*An outburst*) That poor little girl. I can't stand it, I can't stand it . . .[4]

There is Skat, the renegade philanderer, who runs off with Lisa, the smith Plog's somewhat inconstant wide-eyed wife, and, when caught by the angry cuckolded Plog, pulls off the crassly sentimental "death scene," only to be surprised a few minutes later by Death himself, who implacably saws down the tree on which Skat is sitting:

DEATH: I'm sawing down your tree because your time is up.
SKAT: It won't do. I haven't got time.

DEATH: So you haven't got time.
SKAT: No, I have my performance.
DEATH: Then it's canceled because of death.
SKAT: My contract.
DEATH: Your contract is terminated.
SKAT: My children, my family.
DEATH: Shame on you, Skat!
SKAT: Yes, I'm ashamed.

Death begins to saw again. The tree creaks.

SKAT: Isn't there any way to get off? Aren't there any special rules for actors?
DEATH: No, not in this case.
SKAT: No loopholes, no exceptions?

Death saws.

SKAT: Perhaps you'll take a bribe.

Death saws.

SKAT: Help!

Death saws.

SKAT: Help! Help!

The tree falls. The forest becomes silent again.[5]

There is the darker villain, Raval, the vicious seminarian and womanizer, who yet emerges at the awful encounter in the forest as quite simply a pitiable human orphan, without protection from above and abandoned by his fellow mortals whose charity cannot reach out to encompass his awful doomed state for fear of infection to themselves:

RAVAL: Can't you give me a little water? *(Pause)* I have the plague.
JÖNS: Don't come here. If you do I'll slit your throat. Keep to the other side of the tree.
RAVAL: I'm afraid of death.

No one answers. There is complete silence. Raval gasps heavily for air. The dry leaves rustle with his movements.

RAVAL: I don't want to die! I don't want to!

No one answers. Raval's face appears suddenly at the base of the tree. His eyes bulge wildly, and his mouth is ringed with foam.

RAVAL: Can't you have pity on me? Help me! At least talk to me.

No one answers. The trees sigh. Raval begins to cry.

RAVAL: I am going to die. I. I. *I!* What will happen to me! Can no one console me? Haven't you any compassion? Can't you see that I . . .

His words are choked off by a gurgling sound. He disappears in the darkness behind the fallen tree. It becomes quiet for a few moments.

RAVAL (*Whispers*): Can't anyone . . . only a little water.

Suddenly the girl gets up with a quick movement, snatches Jöns' water bag and runs a few steps. Jöns grabs her and holds her fast.

JÖNS: It's no use. It's no use. I know that it's no use. It's meaningless. It's totally meaningless. I tell you that it's meaningless. Can't you hear that I'm consoling you?
RAVAL: Help me, help me!

No one answers, no one moves. Raval's sobs are dry and convulsive, like a frightened child's. His sudden scream is cut off in the middle.
Then it becomes quiet.

Here, then, most dramatically and implacably, as throughout the entire background of this film, the absence of God is articulated as incomparably more and worse than a mere negative philosophical proposition. It is not a robust or optimistic atheism which takes the place of faith. It is Jöns' articulation of total meaninglessness. One thinks of Camus and of the most drastic and consistent and consequential of all atheists, Nietzsche himself. Flagellants lash themselves in a frenzy of penance and no notice is taken; a young deluded witch is seared and charred and no answer comes; a posturing actor tries his turn on the ultimate reality and is promptly silenced without compassion and with reproaches for his bombast; a dying sinner cries out for mercy and not only the absent God but even his fellow human beings decline to answer, though these latter cannot prevent themselves from hearing.

In effect, in this meaningless atheistic universe the only policy that seems to make any sense is Jön's policy of cannily compassionate cynicism and cautious egotism. The knight does indeed make a tremulous beginning at placing a certain shy and bemused trust in human affection and kindness, his own kindness to the juggler's family, whom he invites under his protection for the dangerous journey through the nighttime forest. In fact, the interlude which leads to and concludes with this invitation serves likewise as the symbol bridge to Bergman's next God film, *Wild Strawberries*. But before we inspect this important symbol bridge (one of many which are of utmost importance in properly grasping the dynamic of the film series as a whole) we must consider in detail the basic problematic of *The Seventh Seal* itself.

The Seventh Seal formulates the problematic of the entire film series; and that problematic is the silence of God. The formulation is effected in the confessional scene in the little gray stone church, where the knight, seeking peace in the sacrament of penance, finds at the end that he has been confessing to the black-robed figure of Death hidden behind the grille. It must be noted forthwith in advance that this confessional scene in *The Seventh Seal* foreshadows and is answered by another confessional scene in the last film of our series, *Persona*. In the initial confessional scene, the God-mouthpiece, Death, is obstinately, almost malevolently, certainly impertinently, silent; in the final confessional scene of *Persona*, the God-mouthpiece, the beautiful and mysteriously wordless actress Elizabeth Vogler, is poignantly, almost impotently, certainly meaningfully, silent. The silence of Death in *The Seventh Seal* triggers in both knight and viewer a riot of complex and disturbing emotional reactions: suspicion that Death may in fact have no answers, fear that he may be a malevolent devil bent on torturing, concern that he is simply a superb chess strategist determined to trick his opponent, in the very act of confession, into revealing his prospective moves. The silence of Elizabeth Vogler in *Persona* will infuriate the young nurse Alma but will stun the viewer by its very eloquence; for, by then, we shall know why this supremely symbolic figure, Elizabeth Vogler, she of the many masks, is silent; we shall know this with a profundity and lucidity of insight impossible at the initial point in this film saga in *The Seventh Seal*; and we shall be moved to awe at such terrifying love.

Such is the great arc spanned by the entire series: an initial oppressive uncertainty, an anguished doubt, and a strong hint of total meaninglessness; a terminal horrifying certainty, a heart-rending clarity, and an unmistakable message of meaningfulness which is as horrifying as it is stimulating.

Since *The Seventh Seal* (and indeed the entire film series) is no mere shadowy intellectual morality play, no mere syllogistic exercise in plastic theology, we shall find the problematic in this first film (and in all succeeding ones) multidimensional and complicated. It is the fate of man to be thus complicated, for he is a composite creature, a crossroads creature.

We must have the confessional scene of *The Seventh Seal* before us in its entirety in order to assess the strands of the problematic:

KNIGHT: Through my indifference to my fellow men, I have isolated myself from their company. Now I live in a world of phantoms. I am imprisoned in my dreams and fantasies.

DEATH: And yet you don't want to die?

KNIGHT: Yes, I do.

DEATH: What are you waiting for?

KNIGHT: I want knowledge.

DEATH: You want guarantees?

KNIGHT: Call it whatever you like. Is it so cruelly inconceivable to grasp God with the senses? Why should he hide himself in a mist of half-spoken promises and unseen miracles?

Death doesn't answer.

KNIGHT: How can we have faith in those who believe when we can't have faith in ourselves? What is going to happen to those of us who want to believe but aren't able to? And what is to become of those who neither want to nor are capable of believing?

The Knight stops and waits for a reply, but no one speaks or answers him. There is complete silence.

KNIGHT: Why can't I kill God within me? Why does he live on in this painful and humiliating way even though I curse Him and want to tear Him out of my heart? Why, in spite of everything, is He a baffling reality that I can't shake off? Do you hear me?

DEATH: Yes, I hear you.

KNIGHT: I want knowledge, not faith, not suppositions, but knowledge. I want God to stretch out his hand toward me, reveal Himself and speak to me.

DEATH: But he remains silent.

KNIGHT: I call out to him in the dark but no one seems to be there.

DEATH: Perhaps no one is there.

KNIGHT: Then life is an outrageous horror. No one can live in the face of death, knowing that all is nothingness.

DEATH: Most people never reflect about either death or the futility of life.

KNIGHT: But one day they will have to stand at that last moment of life and look toward the darkness.

DEATH: When *that* day comes . . .

KNIGHT: In our fear, we make an image, and that image we call God.

DEATH: You are worrying . . .

KNIGHT: Death visited me this morning. We are playing chess together. This reprieve gives me the chance to arrange an urgent matter.

DEATH: What matter is that?

KNIGHT: My life has been a futile pursuit, a wandering, a great deal of talk without meaning. I feel no bitterness or self-reproach because the lives of most people are very much like this. But I will use my reprieve for one meaningful deed.[7]

From this tightly packed, highly nuanced dialogue, the cardinal point, the silence of God, is tolerably clear. We must, however, note these vital subsidiary elements:

1. There is the problem of faith and man's psychological

ambivalence in its regard. On the one hand, man demands, as the knight expressly articulates, "knowledge, not faith, not suppositions, but knowledge," and this creates a perhaps unrecognized tension between the genuine ontological reality of faith and the spurious coin of a cowardly certitude. This reality of faith Catholic theologizing has dangerously subverted into little more than intellectual assent to abstract propositions, whereas Protestant thought has more soundly recognized and proclaimed it to be predominantly an anguished personal trust in a personal reality. Job's ultimate outburst is pertinent here: "Though he slay me, yet will I trust in him" (Job 13:15). On the other hand, the knight perfectly expresses man's utter unwillingness and incapacity to "live in the face of death, knowing that all is nothingness." Man is not satisfied with faith as personal trust in a personal God (the knight indeed confuses faith with "suppositions," thus effectively subverting it and robbing it of its quality of personal relationship with a reality personally experienced), and at the same time man is not willing to accept the apparent report of his "knowledge," namely the persuasion that "all is nothingness."

Yet the knight utters one ingenuous cry that must find an echo in any heart not subverted by rationalistic mentalism: "Is it so cruelly inconceivable to grasp God with the senses?" and again: "I call out to him in the dark but no one seems to be there." The real problematic, the insistent and continuing problematic of the entire film series, is this aesthetic problem of nonencounter at the level of the senses. I would venture at once to suggest that there is here a luminous reality in play that has been missed both by the excessively rationalistic Catholics and the excessively emotionalistic Protestants. This reality is the gradually clarifying reality that will dominate the dynamic of these films until it finally emerges into appalling light at the end of *Persona*. This reality is *the speaking God-Man*. Both theological camps pay lip service to this reality, but then each immediately proceeds to circumvent the reality they have posited as fulcrum of the whole of revelation history. The superrationalistic Catholics, after acknowledging that God transcends human reason, proceed to a stringent effort to warp his utterances into propositions that can be comprehended by that reason; they omit all serious consideration of the thrilling and horrifying implications of the fact they themselves proclaim, that God speaks to us in his Son! They are concerned with truths about God as object of man's belief-reaction; they evade the crucial fact ("crucial" in more ways than one!) that man is to respond to quite another truth, the existential truth that is the incarnate God; and that response can only be love or deicide. The superemotionalistic Protestants, after acknowledging that God does indeed speak meaningfully to man, then proceed to demand of man a blind faith in a Person whose mighty personality gradually hardens into the evil arbitrariness of a Calvinistic predestining autocrat. They seem unwilling to face the implications of *kenosis*, of the supreme and courageous creative love that exposes himself to his creatures entirely in a rendezvous at a tree. The reality of the incarnate God saves God's utterance from transcendentalistic arbitrariness; the supremely personal character of this incarnate God obviates all danger of a relapse of the believer into rationalistic parsing of the divine revelation. The response demanded in the Christian dispensation is neither the mere intellectual assent to a series of propositions nor yet the blind faith in an unman, but rather the personal acceptance of a divine person "made man." This, of course, exposes both the believer and the incarnate God to certain risks. But risk is the unavoidable accompaniment of all love that is really free.

2. There is the problem of personal isolation. The knight confesses (and remember that the knight supposes himself throughout this scene to be in the sacramental forum of penance; therefore he is certainly making more than a series of merely descriptive statements about his life and actions and omissions) —the knight, then, *confesses* that he has isolated himself from the company of his fellowmen through his own indifference. The result is that he is now forced to live "in a world of phantoms.

I am imprisoned in my dreams and fantasies." This problematic is simply stated, not further developed here; but the knight's thrust to become involved in and with the fate of Mia and Jof is a clear implementation of his resolve to do that "one meaningful deed" of which he has spoken to his hidden confessor. The theme of personal isolation engendered by personal sluggishness and egotism will be drastically developed in succeeding films.

3. There is the problem of the psychologically ambivalent attitude to God. The knight is immoderately incensed against a mere figment of his own imagination. He rails against the God whom he later describes as an image made by man for all the world as if God were a highly conscious skulker in man's own tormented heart. Moreover, the knight almost pathetically exposes his ambivalence when Death patiently and agreeably informs him: "Perhaps no one is there"; for the knight shouts: "Then life is an outrageous horror"!

4. There is the problem of man's persistent questioning, even in his temperamental atheism. The knight in fact flings out in rapid succession no fewer than eight questions, revealing a thoroughly distraught and disoriented state of mind. For the questions are mutually incompatible: if the meaningfulness of the first two be granted, then there is a God and the succeeding questions about man's (the knight's) inability to kill God within him become pointless; if the first two questions on the other hand be dismissed as meaningless because there is no God, then the succeeding questions become simply silly, at best psychological commentaries on a strange illness! Yet man, epitomized by the knight, does continue to ask such contradictory questions. And a little of the reason should already glimmer here: it is because the God-man relationship is an intensely and painfully personal one, part and parcel of the dark night of loving, of the bloody dialogue between free conscious realities.

Moreover there is an implication in all this questioning that is unacceptable to God. The key to this (and it is vital for the entire saga of these films) is to be found in the most important interchange between the knight and Death during that confessional scene:

KNIGHT: I want knowledge.
DEATH: You want guarantees?

One entire strand of the God-man relationship and drama is relentlessly highlighted in that brief dialogue. God will not give a guarantee that would annihilate man's freedom. In his implacable and divinely loving transcendence God is determined that man shall always preserve the agonizing freedom that will enable him to say with Antonius Block: "This is my hand. I can move it, feel the blood pulsing through it. The sun is still high in the sky and I, Antonius Block, am playing chess with Death." [8] It is precisely the chess motif that stays Death's hand:

KNIGHT: Wait a moment.
DEATH: That's what they all say. I grant no reprieves.
KNIGHT: You play chess, don't you?

A gleam of interest kindles in Death's eyes . . .

DEATH: Yes, in fact I'm quite a good chess player. [9]

Chess is of all human games the most perfect paradigm of the freedom mystery and of the God-man relationship. For chess brings into play an enormous number of possible choices, all of them free and therefore unpredictable; yet the rhythm of the game is such that a player with a perfect grasp of the combinations of possible moves *and of the psychology of his challenger* is bound to win. In this whole film the fitfully played-out game seems indeed a grim one; and only Jof at the very end catches a glimmer of Death's beneficent character precisely as winner:

And Death, the severe master, invites them to dance. . . . They dance away from the dawn and it's a solemn dance toward the dark lands, while the rain washes their faces and cleans the salt of the tears from their cheeks. [10]

And here lies the counterpoint strand of the God-man nexus. If God wills to expose himself as incarnate to answer man's legitimate need to "grasp God with the senses," then this exposure pursues a transcendent purpose, the deification, the apotheosis, of man. "He became man so that we might become Gods." This is no merely humanized God doomed to death so that man may catch up the falling torch of divinity; this God comes in the flesh to demand just that total surrender of the creature that is paradigmed by the surrender of death, so that God can give the radiant new dawn. And when it is given, that dawn is initially so strange to mortal eyes as to seem terrifying. It is a catching up into the very life of God himself, whose "peace" is not as the world's is. Not until we reach the final film *Persona* shall we see just how beautiful can be that God here so somberly portrayed in *The Seventh Seal*—and just how drastically free man can spurn that eternal beauty and board the bus for the paltry despicable little urban settlement he would gladly call his goal and his perfect bliss.

The basic problem strand looms especially oppressively evident at three high points of the film: the knight's confessional scene; the burning of Tyan; the ultimate crisis in the great hall of the knight's castle when Death enters to claim his own. The first of these scenes renders tangible and menacing the crisis of the human heart seeking religious belief and being greeted by a silence; the second manifests the profound dull but devouring horror of man, expressed by the squire in his outburst: "Emptiness, my lord! . . . and our terror and hers are the same"; the final scene nervously pulls together the whole gamut of human emotions in this nihilistic universe as knight and squire antiphonally proclaim the anguish of faltering faith and the bravado of defiant unbelief in the somber *silent* presence of the great lord Death:

> KNIGHT: From our darkness, we call out to Thee, Lord. Have mercy on us because we are small and frightened and ignorant.

JÖNS   *(bitterly):* In the darkness where You are supposed to be, where all of us probably are . . . In the darkness You will find no one to listen to Your cries or be touched by Your sufferings. Wash Your tears and mirror Yourself in Your indifference.

KNIGHT: God, You who are somewhere, who *must* be somewhere, have mercy upon us.

JÖNS: I could have given you an herb to purge you of your worries about eternity. Now it seems to be too late. But in any case, feel the immense triumph of this last moment when you can still roll your eyes and move your toes.

KARIN: Quiet, quiet.

JÖNS: I shall be silent, but under protest.

GIRL   *(on her knees):* It is the end.[11]

A silence has been interpreted by man as evidence of the radical absence of God and therefore of all meaning; man is left alone, still "small and frightened and ignorant" but ineluctably alone; and he can do nothing but "feel the immense triumph" in the penultimate moment of his terminally mortal existence of being able to roll his eyes and move his toes.

This entire syndrome is not presented in order to point up any moral. It is quite simply a presentation of a truth about modern man as Bergman has seen and experienced that truth. No reason or explanation is given for the knight's failure to encounter more than a silence, no hint of a hidden light flashes around poor Tyan's desperate and pathetic funeral pyre; and at the end, Death advances majestically but silently on his victims.

The nihilistic atheism is climaxed in the squire's outburst before Tyan's pyre. The real and ultimate truth, he is insisting, is neither God nor even devil, neither a benign nor a malignant fate, but simply "emptiness under the moon." Yet man is definitely unready and unable to accept this: the squire at once cries out, "That poor little girl. I can't stand it, I can't stand it," and the knight continues long after this searing experience of the burning of Tyan to exclaim, "God, You who are somewhere, who *must* be somewhere, have mercy upon us." Yet outbursts of desperation and cries of anguished appeal alike remain unanswered. Neither knight nor squire—or indeed any of the others, with the exception of little Jof—has any reassuring experience. And as for Jof's experience, two equally important points must be made: it is undeniably part of the total witness of the film, and it mediates no real certitude, no clinching conviction. It simply opens up an avenue the others have not yet found.

But if the human seeker is frustrated in his encounter with God, where shall he seek for the cure for loneliness? His only option is to seek within his fellow mortals for some kind of redemptive love-union; or finally to try to find the satisfaction his soul craves, neurally craves and craves with insistent longing, within himself. If he fails in both dimensions, he will probably quite simply go mad. In succeeding films of the series, man will indeed launch out on the treacherous seas of both dimensions, fellow mortals and narcissistic solipsism. Madness will stalk those later films in various guises. They will explore the dual path always open to man: to seek fulfillment by force, by probing will-to-power, or to seek it by openhearted and courageous love. In some of the films the absence of God will retreat into an almost soporific wistfulness, only to advance again into a challenging and terrifying presence. Always the "argument," the witness, and the manifestation will be at the aesthetic, the neural, level. And always there will be hints, even as in this first film, of a whole dimension (or indeed dimensions) of reality behind the dimension actually portrayed on the screen. Yet these dimensions will remain, until *Persona*, essentially necromantic and dubiously comforting; they will remain chilling and terrifying—and, at very best, a dubious temporary escape from the true horror of empirical reality, which is constantly presented as abysmally dismal, cheerless at the core, a business of faded elegance and meaningless scrabbling after many conflicting ends. And the ultimate component of that atmosphere of futility and pain is superbly etched in the stage directions for the knight's confessional scene (etched in a motif that will recur at a crucial moment in another film):

The knight is kneeling before a small altar. It is dark and quiet around him. The air is cool and musty. Pictures of saints look down on him with stony eyes. Christ's face is turned upward, His mouth open as if in a cry of anguish.[12]

It is beneath this face that Death hears the knight's confession. But that face of Christ is still an unrelated and ultimately irrelevant fact for Antonius Block, the crusading knight. Nothing is stirred in Block's heart but the pity wryly expressed by the squire in his apostrophe: ". . . In the darkness You will find no one to listen to Your cries or be touched by Your sufferings. Wash Your tears and mirror Yourself in Your indifference." Whatever the future course of this film series, we must surely know already that this will be no easy progress, in terms of formula, from intellectual doubt to intellectual certitude, nor yet from emotional abandonment to emotional encounter and satisfaction. This is modern man who simply cannot be satisfied with the relatively easy comforts of a simpler, cruder, and homier age. At best this man sees spiders (as we shall desperately see a spider through the madness-tormented eyes of a sick girl in a later film of the series); at worst he sees "emptiness under the moon." And we must begin to realize that man himself must somehow drive forward and be driven forward to a more desperate rendezvous than a mere Sunday school encounter with the loving Savior. Indeed the ultimate encounter in *Persona* will be a profound emotional experience, but it will have horror flickering around its edges, the horror of man as he dimly realizes he can kill, has killed, God his Savior. In the beginning odyssey, furthermore, there are two voyagers: God and man. Both will travel a lonely path, rarely together, mostly at odds; and the final encounter will highlight that freedom which is beyond appeal, that freedom that poses the real problem and renders possible the dichotomy of the answer, an answer which is perennially uncertain as long as man remains free, that is, as long as man remains man.

In *The Seventh Seal* the God-mouthpiece, Death, is inscrutable, silent at the most inopportune moments, only faintly and wryly humorous. Yet this mouthpiece hints at certain major themes later to be explicated. For instance, Death has a significant interchange with Block after defeating him in the intermittent chess game:

> DEATH: . . . When we meet again, you and your companions' time will be up.
> KNIGHT: And you will divulge your secrets.
> DEATH: I have no secrets.
> KNIGHT: So you know nothing.
> DEATH: I have nothing to tell.[13]

There is nothing pertaining to the inner essence of this inscrutable wanderer that can be told in human terms. For that telling there must be an existential passage: either of man to the lands called dark by human viewers; or of God to a terrible rendezvous in the flesh.

Again, at the very outset, in their first encounter, the God-mouthpiece of *The Seventh Seal* identifies himself:

> KNIGHT: Who are you?
> DEATH: I am Death.
> KNIGHT: Have you come for me?
> DEATH: I have been walking by your side for a long time.[14]

"I am the Resurrection and the Life," says the Gospel Christ. "I am Death," says Bergman's God, the Death that must precede that resurrection for you mortals if you would put on immortality, if you would really learn to speak my language. For no matter how respectful I may be of your freedom, no matter how demanding I may be upon your responsibility, no matter how solicitous I may be of your dignity, we can never abolish the fact that I am your Creator. If you will not relate to me in this light, then you must inevitably put me on the mantel as a piece of animistic bric-a-brac.

Finally, at the end of the film, Death again is silent; yet it is a majestic silence, and the awesomeness of his presence ennobles every mortal on whom his shadow falls, even the clumsy smith Plog. It is part of the exquisite irony of this last scene that the distracted and desperate knight, crying out to "God, You who are somewhere," is at that very moment standing in the shadow of the God he has sought and fought and finally found, without knowing it and without realizing all the pain and all the happiness that this finding must involve.

No, at the end of *The Seventh Seal* man has found no redemptive answer to his dread and his loneliness. Man's theoaesthetic quest has faltered into paralysis before the implacable countenance of Death. But man has made a slight move in the direction of another sort of seeking after the answer to his loneliness and his longing. I am firmly persuaded after a most careful review of these seven films and their intermeshing motifs that no symbol employed by Bergman is ever entirely arbitrary or even used in one single vacuum-type situation. Therefore the symbol bridge in *The Seventh Seal*, that symbol bridge that points to the next film, is of more than passing significance.

When the knight has chanced upon the little juggler's family, Mia has told him, "I picked a basket of wild strawberries this afternoon. And we have a drop of milk fresh from a cow." [15] The repetition is insistent, as Mia gives the strawberries to the knight and Jof with the remark: "These are wild strawberries from the forest. I have never seen such large ones. They grow up there on the hillside. Notice how they smell!" [16]

Stimulated by this simple act of hospitality and this pastoral interlude, the knight makes his own kindly suggestion of human solidarity in the face of the nighttime dangers of the woods. And he sums up his impressions thus:

> I shall remember this moment. The silence, the twilight, the bowls of strawberries and milk, your faces in the evening light. . . . I'll carry this memory between my hands as carefully as if it were a bowl filled to the brim with fresh milk. . . . And it will be an adequate sign—it will be enough for me. [17]

In the next film, *Wild Strawberries*, which takes its title from this fragment of conversation, we shall be introduced into an environment in which man tries to forget entirely the God he has sought in vain and endeavors instead to find happiness in the dimension of sheer mortality, only to find himself frustrated by his own inveterate callousness and cowardice.

The Seventh Seal is the last in the Apocalypse to be broken by the Lamb; and its breaking causes a silence to ensue in heaven "for about the space of half an hour." It is the silence of a God who can only achieve the revelation intended by some drastic and risky magic. Somehow God and man must be made able to speak the same language.

QUESTING

Wild Strawberries

Where is the friend I seek everywhere?

Wild Strawberries is the story of "the events, dreams and thoughts which befell"[1] old Isak Borg, Doctor of Medicine, on the day he traveled to Lund to receive an honorary degree. We at once discover that Borg's wife is dead and he is living at uneasy daggers-drawn with his fussy housekeeper, Agda, who idolizes and spoils him but has tantrums of offended dignity when she feels herself slighted. Borg has one son, Evald, married to a spirited girl, Marianne. This daughter-in-law has come to stay with Borg for a few days in the hopes he might help her and Evald in their marital problems. Briefly, Evald has insisted that Marianne abort the child she has conceived of him because he does not believe in bringing children into a meaningless world; in fact Evald wants only to be dead himself. Borg has curtly refused to get involved.

In the car en route for Lund, Marianne bitterly reproaches

her father-in-law for his callousness and also for his lack of all paternal feeling: Borg has lent Evald money but at staggeringly high interest rates. They reach the house where Borg used to live. Marianne goes for a swim, and Isak Borg penetrates into a strange half-world of his childhood as he approaches the house and sees his childhood sweetheart cousin Sara picking wild strawberries. As unbidden and invisible guest at a birthday party that actually occurred many years ago, Isak hears Sara tell what an impossible prig he, Isak, is and hint at her incipient romance with his brother Sigfrid. He wakes to present-day reality to find a girl standing beside him who introduces herself likewise as Sara, one of a group of three young people hitchhiking to Italy. Her companions are Viktor, an atheistic medical student, and Anders, a sentimental student for the Lutheran ministry. Isak and Marianne give them a lift. Soon the car collides with one inexpertly driven by Berit Alman, who hates her husband and taunts him constantly as Borg's car, now somewhat overcrowded, resumes its journey with the Almans jammed in to be taken to a garage to get help. The Alman argument becomes so violent that Marianne orders the couple out of the car. They drive on to an inn, where they stop for dinner and a theological discussion. Isak, accompanied by Marianne, leaves the three youngsters for a while to visit his ancient mother who lives nearby. After a chilling and most revealing encounter with the old lady, Marianne and Borg rejoin the young people and drive on. Isak dozes off as the car, now driven by Marianne, cruises on. He slips into another strange encounter with his cousin Sara and an even stranger and more terrifying trial scene where he is himself the accused and Alman a mysterious sort of judge. The trial has to do with Borg's own marriage, and we learn how loveless he had been toward his wife. This dreadful scene, which ends in Isak's being condemned to the supreme penalty of loneliness, merges into another brief encounter with cousin Sara, and Isak awakes in the stopped car: the youngsters have insisted on going to gather flowers to pay homage to Isak on his honorary degree day. Marianne now tells Isak in detail the horrible tale of her troubles with the death-seeking Evald. The flowers are duly presented and a few more hours' drive brings the party to Lund. A tentative reconciliation is sketched between Evald and Marianne, and Isak prepares for the degree-conferring ceremony at which he restlessly analyzes his strange experiences of the day without arriving at any clarity. Home again, he talks briefly and awkwardly with Evald, trying to establish some kind of more paternal relation to his son. Evald shrugs this off stiffly, but Marianne tells her father-in-law she loves him. The old man slips again into the dream world of his remembered childhood, with the pervasive scent of wild strawberries dominating his dream consciousness.

This is a film analysis of restrictive humanism and a somber investigation of the death in life of a hidebound and comfort-conscious old egotist who only tremulously learns at film's end how dead he is and what faint hope may exist for a revivification. Its immediate juxtaposition to *The Seventh Seal* recalls André Malraux's remark in the early postwar years to a group of young European intellectuals: "The question is no longer whether God is dead. The question today in this old land of Europe is whether man is dead."

Superficially, and in terms of scenario, incomparably less somber and malignant than *The Seventh Seal*, *Wild Strawberries* is, upon deeper penetration, far more horrifying: for we find man truly dead in his little humanistic house that was supposed to be so cozy; and we glimpse the first intrusion, via the dream sequences, of that other world behind the wallpaper of this bourgeois humanistic home. If anyone had imagined that the terminal disappointment of *The Seventh Seal* would engender a brave and tender atheistic humanism, he must be entirely disabused of any such pious fancy by this succeeding film, *Wild Strawberries*. For here again Bergman is telling the truth about modern man as he sees that truth, telling it and compelling us to experience it, as always, at the aesthetic, neural level. Silence of God and God-mouthpiece will emerge in this film in due time and in especially disturbing form. But the overall thrust and theme is simply lovelessness. If atheism of doubt and numb nonencounter are typical of modern man, Bergman is saying to us in this film that lovelessness is equally typical of that same modern man, typical precisely of modern man's finest and most respected sort of representative, the honored old physician and healer Isak Borg, who cannot heal himself, who scarcely wants to heal himself.

Before addressing ourselves to a detailed study of the unfolding saga of modern man in this strange film, we may usefully sum up in point form the developing thrust of the series. Man has no meaningful contact with God, said *The Seventh Seal*; man is loveless, says *Wild Strawberries*. At a similar point in each new chapter of the saga we shall recall the developing thrust and add the new dimension of each succeeding film.

Isak's self-identification as a typical humanistic egotist comes in a lengthy soliloquy at the outset of the film:

> . . . I have of my own free will withdrawn almost completely from society. . . . Therefore I have found myself rather alone in my old age. This is not a regret but a statement of fact. All I ask of life is to be left alone and to have the opportunity to devote myself to the few things which continue to interest me, however superficial they may be. . . . Perhaps I ought to add that I am an old pedant, and at times quite trying, both to myself and to the people who have to be around me. I detest emotional outbursts, women's tears and the crying of children. On the whole, I find loud noises and sudden startling occurrences most disconcerting.[2]

Isak goes on to recount a particularly horrible dream he has had recently. The nub of the dream is Isak's encounter with his own corpse:

> I stood alone with the overturned, partly smashed coffin. Gripped by a fearful curiosity, I approached. A hand stuck out from the pile of splintered boards. When I leaned forward, the dead hand clutched my arm and pulled me down toward the casket with enormous force. I struggled helplessly against it as the corpse slowly rose from the coffin. It was a man dressed in a frock coat.

To my horror, I saw that the corpse was myself. I tried to free my arm, but he held it in a powerful grip. All this time he stared at me without emotion and seemed to be smiling scornfully.

In this moment of senseless horror, I awakened and sat up in my bed.[3]

But old Isak is no isolated monster of egotism and moribund, death-lusting humanity in the world of this film. The all-pervading lovelessness emerges in progressively wider circles as Marianne tells Isak about her interview with Evald when Evald demanded the abortion:

It's absurd [Evald had protested] to live in this world, but it's even more ridiculous to populate it with new victims and it's most absurd of all to believe that they will have it any better than us.[4]

Marianne certainly represents, during this scene with Evald, the positive-minded courageous human fighter, but her husband immediately exposes a still deeper reason for his own pessimism and thereby centers his own dilemma within the circle of the chief offender, his father Isak:

Personally I was an unwelcome child in a marriage which was a nice imitation of hell. Is the old man really sure that I'm his son? Indifference, fear, infidelity and guilt feelings—those were my nurses.[5]

The Evald-Marianne conversation terminates with a chilling interchange highlighting the full horror of despairing humanistic pessimism unrelieved by a single glimmer of hope:

MARIANNE: I know that you're wrong.
EVALD: There is nothing which can be called right or wrong. One functions according to one's needs; you can read that in an elementary-school textbook.
MARIANNE: And what do we need?
EVALD: You have a damned need to live, to exist and to create life.
MARIANNE: And how about you?
EVALD: My need is to be dead. Absolutely, totally dead.[6]

In dramatic counterpitted manifestos, this exchange makes explicit the diametric opposition between a human being who lives in the spirit (if not in the faith!) of the living God and a human being who lives in the shadow of pessimistic autonomy. If Marianne scarcely believes in God, she still reverences the new life she carries within her, and this makes her in some sense a creationist rather than a nihilist.

Isak and Marianne's visit to his old mother is absolutely vital to the God-dynamic of the series, and we shall return to it in detail later. But this encounter among Isak, his ancient withered mother, and his terrified young daughter-in-law sketches in a few bold strokes still another dimension of lovelessness. Marianne sums up the impressions of the encounter in an outburst that is simultaneously a horrifying diagnosis of the fundamental disease of lovelessness and consequent hopelessness afflicting the chief characters in this film and a vibrant protest against that lovelessness by a young woman who emerges as a guardian of life and champion of the proposition that to exist is better than not to exist and that to exist is to love:

> When I saw you together with your mother, I was gripped by a strange fear. . . . I thought, here is his mother. A very ancient woman, completely ice-cold, in some ways more frightening than death itself. And here is her son, and there are light-years of distance between them. And he himself says that he is a living death. And Evald is on the verge of becoming just as lonely and cold— and dead. And then I thought that there is only coldness and death, and death and loneliness, all the way. Somewhere it must end.[7]

The champion of life is herself distraught with horror at the vision of her world; and though at the end of the film she seems to have won a tenuous victory, with Evald consenting to do what she wants in the matter of the child, there is a subtle disturbing hint that by this time Marianne may herself have become infected with Evald's pessimism, or rather that her undoubted love for her husband may have caused her to consider at least turning traitor to life itself and creeping into his vicious little tent of egotistical autonomy where dwells a totally independent mortal permeated by utter hopelessness.

If Isak at film's end seems to be groping toward some issue out of his damned and lonely egotism, it is certainly in no small part due to the horrible dream experience he has had en route, where he has been put on trial for the supreme lovelessness—to his own wife. The trial takes place in a phantasmagoric setting peopled by ghosts from Isak's youth and the loveless husband, Alman, to whom he has given a lift after a near-fatal crash. The dream sequence reveals to Isak the real reason for his wife's inconstancy and infidelity: his own utter coldness. And the trial places the old doctor squarely before the great challenge to, the supreme demand levied on, egotistical man. For the first, but by no means the last, time in these films an inscription in a radically unknown and unidentifiable tongue challenges the seeker with a conundrum which it is most urgent for him to resolve. It is as if God were setting the riddle and demanding that man learn the correct language to answer it: not that this language is necessarily univocally God-tongue; but it is certainly at least the language Pope John was thinking of when, on his deathbed, he told his English teacher, "So we didn't make much headway, did we? But it doesn't matter now. Where I am going, they speak only one language, the language of love." The inscription confronting Dr. Isak Borg in the strange courtroom reads:

INKE TAN MAGROV

STAK FARSIN LOS

KRET FAJNE KASERTE

MJOTRON PRESETE

and his judge must help him decipher it to read:

A doctor's first duty *is to ask forgiveness.*[8]

And the same doctrinaire implacable judge relentlessly guides Isak forward to an understanding of his own plight and penalty:

ISAK: And what is the penalty?
ALMAN: Penalty? I don't know. The usual one, I suppose.

ISAK: The usual one?
ALMAN: Of course. Loneliness.
ISAK: Loneliness?
ALMAN: Exactly. *Loneliness.*
ISAK: Is there no grace?
ALMAN: Don't ask me. I don't know anything about such things.[9]

Each episode of the dream encounter between Isak and his young love, Sara, is permeated by the lush redness and unique tang of wild strawberries. When Isak first sees her in his strange half dream, Sara is busily picking wild strawberries; when he hails her she takes no notice but continues to pick wild strawberries and put them into a little straw basket; in the upheaval of the amorous encounter between Sara and Sigfrid which the time-traveler Isak must witness, the basket of wild strawberries is knocked over; and in their last sad and disturbing dream encounter, Isak and Sara are again in the presence of the same symbol, for between them stands a little woven basket filled with wild strawberries, even as around them lies a strange silent motionless twilight heavy with dull expectations.

Wild strawberries in *The Seventh Seal* were a symbol of simple human kindness, of willing exposure of the human heart to the heart of another mortal, of hospitality and involvement. These are the very qualities that Isak has never shown, in his proud fastidious retreat into the tent of his own comfortable egotism. And so the wild strawberries are spilled and his chance of love is missed. Thus far, in the light of the mere fact that Sara chooses Sigfrid rather than Isak, it might seem to be simply bad luck in love for Isak, that bad luck that can dog the finest person; but Isak gives ample proof throughout the ensuing years that the root of his ill fortune goes much deeper, lies ultimately in a fundamental sluggishness of the heart engendered by his own egocentricity. With mother, wife, son, and daughter-in-law in turn, he displays the same aloof cautious coldness. His increasingly frantic search to recapture his lost youth develops rapidly into a search for the wild strawberries of spontaneous outgoing human affection. Isak learns in pain and terror a lesson that just may not have come to him too late: that in order to love, one must be courageous and generous; that in order to be loved, one must love; that in order to receive, one must give and give unstintingly. But this is precisely what the aged doctor finds it so terrifyingly difficult to do. He makes a first pathetic step, poignant in its very paltriness, when Marianne has finished relating the story of Evald. In the past, Isak has specifically forbidden the young woman to smoke cigarettes, for he can't stand the smoke and further considers the habit expensive and unhealthy; now he tells her simply that she may smoke a cigarette if she wants to.

God figures quite prominently in the conversation of the three young people, Sara, Viktor, and Anders, who are also, in their own younger and more resilient way, part and parcel of the thoroughly bourgeois universe of *Wild Strawberries*. Viktor and Anders are constantly arguing about the existence of God, as Sara pertly recounts:

> When you left they were talking away about the existence of God. Finally they got so angry that they began shouting at each other. Then Anders grabbed Viktor's arm and tried to twist it off, and Viktor said that was a pretty lousy argument for the existence of God. Then I said that I thought they could skip God and pay some attention to me for a while instead, and then they said that I could stop babbling because I didn't understand that it was a debate of principles, and then I said that whether there was a God or not, they were real wet blankets. Then I left and they ran down the hill to settle things because each of them insisted that the other had hurt his innermost feelings. So now they're going to slug it out.[10]

This is a perfect paradigm of the argumentative man of principle, whether earnest theologian (like Anders) or doctrinaire scientist (like Viktor). Such men have entirely lost touch with the living reality of God and are arguing about personally touted principles of logical reasoning. It is, startlingly enough, old Isak who gently reproves and corrects their brash argumentation when they appeal to him for a judgment on the reality of God and Isak replies by softly and dreamily citing a poem in which Anders and Marianne join in:

Where is the friend I seek everywhere?
Dawn is the time of loneliness and care.
When twilight comes I am still yearning
Though my heart is burning, burning.
I see His trace of glory and power,
In an ear of grain and the fragrance of flower,
In every sign and breath of air.
His love is there.
His voice whispers in the summer breeze.[11]

No single scene of *Wild Strawberries* more tellingly highlights the theoaesthetic dimension of God-searching as against the merely theological one. The knight reached out his hand in the dark and called to God but got no answer; Isak is speaking here of an equally theoaesthetic searching, for a God who will satisfy not the curiosity of the human intelligence but the loneliness of the human heart. But we must likewise note how the scene has changed: man has opted for the autonomy of mortality with its consequent hopelessness, and God lingers on simply as a dimly felt lack, sought after almost absentmindedly as an element needed for the completeness and integrity of the pattern of a childhood playpen or a bourgeois living room.

In the context of such a universe old Mrs. Borg, Isak's mother, pitiably and terrifyingly articulates the uselessness of a God superannuated and retired to lonely if dignified seclusion in a room reminiscent of many an atrophied church, with many beautiful and expensive paintings on the walls and heavy draperies covering the doors. In this distressing setting, God articulates his problems in these latter days:

His creatures have simply forgotten him and neglect him:

> Ten children, and all of them dead except Isak. Twenty grandchildren. None of them visits me except Evald, once a year. It's quite all right—I don't complain—but I have fifteen great-grandchildren whom I've never seen. I send letters and presents for fifty-three birthdays and anniversaries every year. I get kind thank-you notes, but no one visits me except by accident or when someone needs a loan. I am tiresome, of course.[12]

His creatures are impatient of his demise so that they may come totally into their heritage, their inheritance:

> And then I have another fault. I don't die. The inheritance doesn't materialize according to the nice, neat schedules made up by smart young people.[13]

God is seriously faced with the problem of entirely self-sufficient creatures who apparently need nothing from him; he puzzles over what to give them, frantically and a little querulously:

> Look here for a moment. Sigbritt's eldest boy will be fifty. I'm thinking of giving him my father's old gold watch. Can I give it to him, even though the hands have loosened? It is so difficult to find presents for those who have everything.[14]

God realizes that he knows better than these creatures, but the fact remains that they will not listen or allow him even to express an opinion:

> I think that this is Benjamin's locomotive because he was always so amused by trains and circuses and such things. I suppose that's why he became an actor. We quarreled often about it because I wanted him to have an honest profession. And I was right. He didn't make it. I told him that several times. He didn't believe me, but I was right. It doesn't pay much to talk.[15]

There is a dull barrier of misunderstanding between God and his creature, man, which God accepts stolidly but not entirely without pain:

> Hagbart's tin soldiers. I never liked his war games. He was shot while hunting moose. We never understood each other.[16]

Activism and humanistic autonomy have rendered God obsolete and shriveled even formalistic courtesy calls by his creatures to the absolute minimum:

> Now you have to go so that you'll have time for all the things you must do.[17]

Wild Strawberries pictures a questing for escape from loneliness and lovelessness in a universe essentially operatively devoid of God. In a scene which did not appear in the finished film, there is a bishop come to Lund to receive an honorary degree with Isak Borg and the former professor of Roman law, Carl-Adam Tiger. But what an odd conversation develops between Bishop Jakob Hovelius and Isak:

ISAK: Do you remember how in our youth we fought with each other on what we called the metaphysical questions?
JAKOB: How could I forget?
ISAK: And what do you believe now?
JAKOB: I'll tell you, I've ceased thinking about all that.[18]

The universe of *Wild Strawberries* is much gayer and cozier than that of *The Seventh Seal*. The world of Isak's youth radiates bourgeois contentment. But always underneath is the sense of undefinable loss and terror, culminating in the grim scene that ends the dream visit of Isak to his own long-lost adolescence:

> The sky turned black above the sea and large birds circled overhead, screeching toward the house, which suddenly seemed ugly and poor. There was something fateful and threatening in this twilight, in the crying of the child, in the shrieking of the black birds.[19]

And even as *Wild Strawberries* takes its title from its predecessor, so it itself leads into and suggests the very title for its successor, *The Magician*. For the aged doctor emeritus can only be saved by some sort of storming and penetration of another dimension, that of his too long lost youth when he had not yet allowed his heart to become entirely atrophied. And as the film *Wild Strawberries* progresses, the interpenetration of the two dimensions, the bleak comfortless dimension of everyday just underlying the superficial comfort of stuffed sofas and the dread dimension of the lost world of the heart, becomes more and more disturbingly drastic, culminating in the farewell-to-Sara scene already mentioned. In *The Magician*, the questing for an existence free of lovelessness on the part of a man (Isak) who is passively projected into the lost dimension will be supplanted by the professional efforts of an active magician (Albert Emanuel Vogler) who will try to tear the curtain away between the two dimensions.

The universe of *Wild Strawberries*, then, is a transitional universe, midway between the threatening but integral universe of medieval faith and doubt (*The Seventh Seal*) and the terrifying and evil universe of nineteenth-century mesmerism (*The Magician*). In *Wild Strawberries* there have been noticeable shifts: Death, external, passionless, and not devoid of benign humor in *The Seventh Seal*, has metamorphosed into an internal cancer in *Wild Strawberries*, destructive and malign because now no longer prevailing as man's natural passage gate into the dark lands but rather hanging like a hope-destroying pall over his absolutely terminal mortality; and this death is in man now as a willed atrophy of the heart, as cramping and killing egotism and pessimism.

Love has been mocked in *The Seventh Seal* by the compassionate cynic Jöns, but love in that universe still had meaning of a sort: a girl could be stirred to pity for the dying renegade Raval, Jöns could remain loyal to the knight despite all his grumbling, Karin could welcome her husband gravely home and unite her love with his in defense against the dark and somber visitor to their castle. But in *Wild Strawberries*, love has been ungodded completely: it is lust in Isak's wife's lover, baffled desperation in the wife herself, atrophied comfortableness in Isak, erotic need in Evald, mutual laceration in Alman and his hysterical wife; and in Isak's mother it is a commodity soured because it has stood so long unused.

And something else is beginning to emerge ominously. Where before there had been the oppressive silence of the God dimension, that wide door that was empty and gave onto emptiness under the moon, now there is the uneasy stirring of a new or newly discovered dimension, man's own subconscious with its own unresolved problematic. In *Wild Strawberries* this subconscious is still relatively well disciplined, erupting only in dreams and in accesses of remorse and self-accusation. But in the wings is waiting a magician who will imperiously seek to batter down the wall separating that subconscious from everyday life. In the darkness at the corner of the narrow street lurk strange shapes about to stir into menacing life. The withdrawal of God has opened strange passageways for demons.

Restrictive humanism has been tried and found wanting, found to be a restrictive prisonhouse where man languishes in a death of his own making. For man, who craved unsuccessfully for immortality and divine love, cannot banish his own longings by denying their ability to be realized, to be achieved. Torn loose from their moorings, by the curse of doubt and the loss of the age of faith, these longings are about to range loose over barren and blasted heaths, lonely frightening moors, rustling wolf-infested forests. This too is part and parcel of modern man.

The seventh seal has been broken and man has found no certain haven; the wild strawberries of merely human loving have been spilled by human passion, greed, and cautious egotism. It now remains for the magician to try his luck at wresting meaning from the outer dark; but this he can do only by liberating powers that may prove too strong for him and destroy him and his fellows.

If there is one indubitable message emerging from this powerful series of ever more somber films it is the contention that atheism does not bring automatic release for man, that man's heart is indeed a lonely hunter and tends to consider everything its prey, even God, when once it has faltered in its adherence to God. This faltering is never pilloried in moralistic terms; it is only the ultimate deicide in *Persona* that merits such pillorying and is going to get it. For the moment man has embarked on the dangerous adventure of trying to make his own meaning.

Man has not expanded his horizons by the conscious elimination of God; he has merely opened up the limitless dark. Modern man must face the reality of his own dissatisfaction, lovelessness, sluggishness, and instability, on pain of bagatellizing his situation with false comfort that can only lead to disaster.

But how shall man face that complex picture of hidden springs of action and hidden dangers of passion? Initially he will attempt himself to play God in the most dangerous way possible, attempting to gain over his fellow mortals who do not love him, who in fact fear and hate and despise and use him, the sort of controlling power he has imagined God to have been at least alleged to exercise over him, while all the time there was nothing there, no God, only emptiness under the moon. Such a vacuum cries out to be filled; such a power gap clamors for a circuit-closing; the switch will be thrown and the dark powers of unbridled man will ride the night.

The malfeasance of institutional religion in *Wild Strawberries*, as typified in the young Anders about to become a minister of the gospel and old Bishop Hovelius who has ceased to think about such things, is not that it has mistakenly articulated (though it may have done that too) but primarily that it has turned aside from the living reality to the sterile proposition, the unavailing syllogism, has tried to prove by arm-twisting.

The malfeasance of man, as epitomized in Evald and Isak, is not that he has failed to find in creation a meaning that will entirely satisfy his questing mind; it is rather that he has refused to face the apparent meaninglessness, the call to courageous adventure, with a strong and generous heart. Man has indeed legitimately concluded at the neural level that a silence is frustrating his attempts at childlike communication with God; but he has failed to take the next step (only Marianne, and she only in a desultory and addled fashion, has taken that step at all); and that step is to strike out into the darkness with the resolve to love in the dark. Because man has allowed his mind to dominate his heart, he has ended in sterile nihilism simply because the cosmos obviously contains freedom and with freedom comes peril. The peril cannot be charmed away into apt and mechanically operative syllogisms; it can only be borne by the willing heart, and this bearing is the quintessence of love. Because man will not (and if man continues to refuse to), then Another will be compelled to bear that burden of freedom; and this spectacle we shall see in *Persona*. But between lies all the turmoil engendered by man's continuing struggle to evade the struggle. Several panaceas will man seek until at last he is greeted by the ultimate silence, wherein his own mind can no longer articulate any reason for existence and his heart is set only on lacerating reality in simple revenge for reality's being there! More and more objectively meaningless will man's efforts become; and as they become more and more meaningless, so will they engender more and more evil. Even man's decent initiatives will bring ruin on himself and his fellows. Innocence will be more and more cruelly exposed to the inexpert would-be lord of the world. This is the perspective now stretching before us. But for the moment we are still in the antechamber of horrors, the quietly desperate world of Isak Borg.

For a moment we must return to the world of the knight and the squire and once more insistently pose the question, from the theistic point of view, why could or did God not answer them? The most adequate answer is the simplest and most eloquent one: because he was determined that they grow up. And this in no mere humanistically progressive sense. It was not merely that they were to "put away childish things" and shoulder their own responsibility (though that too they were intended to do). But, above all, it was that they were to grow up into gods, to cross the dark lands to the final dawn. Later in the series of films this theme of the unutterability of God's inmost secrets will emerge into center foreground. For the moment be it simply noted that the friendly embrace for which they longed, had it indeed been forthcoming, would simply not have been the embrace of God. You might as well ask the meditative guru to embrace the tiny flea that crawls diligently along his arm and marvels at the sheer size of the cosmos! The point is that the God who cannot, will not, embrace even the anguished knight cannot, will not, be relevant to the lustful egotists of *Wild Strawberries*. For the worst and most horrible of lusts is the lust for security.

Thus man in *Wild Strawberries*, having persuaded himself that God is an irrelevant dream, seeks with wistful sadness for a friend when he should be busy exposing himself to a transforming Creator. Later, much later, this Creator will come to the much-sought rendezvous with his creature man. For the moment we have only the spilled essence of the wild strawberries.

Apart from the two grim scenes of the trial of Isak in the dimension of fantasy dreaming and the argument between Evald and Marianne (in which, note well how Evald stresses "need") in the rain-swept car in the dimension of fact, *Wild Strawberries* radiates preeminently an air of gentle sadness, almost nostalgia, the kind of satin weariness typical of rueful sofas in bourgeois rooms. Man is by no means in open rebellion or convulsive tumult; rather he is in a state of quiet desperation, reconciled, it would seem, to his own terminal mortality; and if there are Isaks left in loneliness and old abandoned mothers neglected in the dimension of affection, there are certainly also pert young healthy Saras, beguiling in their ineffable silliness and sauciness. There are even still the earnest young theology student and the equally earnest young scientist-rebel against all theology and all religion. Perhaps one brief passage of Isak's descriptive reminiscence on the honorary degree ceremony itself most perfectly tethers and skewers this world of dusty, musty middle-class stagnation:

> The ceremonial lecture was dull (as usual). The whole thing went on endlessly (as usual) and the garland girls had to go out and relieve themselves in the little silver pot in the sacristy. But we adults unfortunately had to stay where we were. As you know, culture provides us with these moments of refined torture. Professor Tiger looked as if he were dying, my friend the Bishop fell asleep, and more than one of those present seemed ready to faint. Even our behinds, which have withstood long academic services, lectures, dusty dissertations and dull dinners, started to become numb and ache in silent protest. . . . After the ceremony there was a banquet, but I really felt too tired to go.[20]

And over it all hangs the ominous, though equally accepted, dictum of Schopenhauer, cited by the aged Bishop:

> "Dreams are a kind of lunacy and lunacy a kind of dream." But life is also supposed to be a kind of dream, isn't it? Draw your own conclusion.[21]

PROBING

The Magician

He calls you down; he calls you forth.

Albert Emanuel Vogler, mesmerist and magician extraordinary, is traveling through a forest just south of Stockholm in July of the year 1846. Together with his wife, Manda, disguised as a young male assistant and going by the name of Aman, his "business manager," Tubal, and his ancient grandmother (Granny), he is being driven by the coachman, Simson, toward the capital city and an extremely uncertain future. Perhaps he will get the long-hoped-for opportunity of performing at the Royal Palace; perhaps he will be thrown into prison, for the little troupe has had a checkered career indeed; engagements by the Catholics in Ascona to perform miracles; consequent expulsion as heretics when Tubal presented the bill for their invented miracles and dubious cures of pilgrims; various equally dubious mesmeric and "magnetic" miracles and feats of magic

57

in several towns; a lamentable contratemps in Ostende, where their tricks backfired when the mayor grew cuckold's horns and Vogler was fined, Granny flogged, and Tubal clapped into jail; a shady history of touting miracle remedies, love potions, and charms.

In the forest they chance on and take into their carriage a broken-down and dying actor, Spegel, who collapses and apparently expires just as they reach the tollhouse, where they are suavely but firmly invited into the home of Consul Abraham Egerman. Here a sort of self-appointed investigating committee is waiting to inspect their credentials: there is the pale, irregular-featured royal counselor on medicine, Anders Vergérus; the chubby, wavy-haired chief of police, Frans Starbeck; and the baby-faced consul himself. After some veiled insults in the form of probing questions, which provoke Vogler to blind rage, Starbeck promises the necessary permit for "magnetic performances" in Stockholm on condition that Vogler give a private performance of his program the next morning in the Egerman home. Meantime the magician's troupe is invited to spend the night at Egerman's, having supper in the kitchen.

In the kitchen Tubal begins flattering the ample cook, Sofia, and gets more than he bargained for, since Sofia is definitely looking for someone to warm her widowed bed; Sara, the cheekier of the two young housemaids, wants her fortune told and negotiates for a love potion from the always obliging Tubal, while Sanna, the younger maid, cowers and whimpers in fright before this strange troupe; Simson, Vogler's coachman, takes young Sara off to the laundry room for fieldwork in the wake and power of the love potion; Vogler and Manda retire early, and Rustan, the Egerman footman, is left bewildered at the weird events and undercurrents, together with Antonsson, the Egerman coachman, old Granny having padded out to Sanna's room to sing the frightened girl to sleep. This accomplished, Granny patters back down through the hot, tense night, scribbling a sign on the courtyard wall and muttering a strange incantation. The laundry room couple are busy and do not hear or see a pale figure staggering around in the yard; Antonsson and Rustan, chatting about the strange magician's troupe, are suddenly surprised and horrified by the irruption into the kitchen of a huge flickering figure with inhuman features. The intruder hurls an ax through the darkness that ensues when the draft blows out the lamp; when Rustan and Antonsson come to their senses, the brandy jug has vanished.

Granny briefly visits Manda and Volger, who are unpacking and arranging apparatus for the performance. Egerman's pathetic and hysterical wife, Ottilia, comes to visit Vogler and tells him of her sorrow at the loss of her little daughter; unaware that her husband is listening behind the drapery, she pleads with Vogler to explain why the child died; soon she is inviting Vogler to visit her later in the night when her husband will be drugged with the sleeping potion she has given him with his last drink.

Even as she departs, we discover who was the ghostly intruder and brandy stealer. Spegel the actor steps into Vogler's room, proclaiming that he is not yet quite dead but already in a state of decomposition; after a brief significant dialogue with Vogler, Spegel slips to the floor and Vogler lowers the lifeless body into a black casket forming part of his gear.

Vergérus comes to visit Manda, remarking on the "strange magnetic miracle" that has apparently changed her sex, since she is now no longer disguised. He propositions her to leave Vogler, but she refuses. Vogler, who has been briefly out of the room, returns and almost attacks Vergérus, who reassures him that his wife's faithfulness "borders on madness" and departs.

A long, bitter, desperate reminiscence follows between Vogler and Manda about their strange, partly disreputable, partly terrifyingly preternatural experiences together in the magician's trade. Vogler expresses his absolute hate for all his baiters.

Ottilia is surprised when her late night-visitor turns out to be not Vogler but her own husband. She has told Vogler that their marriage collapsed after the death of the child; now Egerman strikes his wife, then begs her forgiveness.

At ten o'clock the next morning all is ready for the performance. In addition to the Egermans and Vergérus and Starbeck, another person has come to witness the performance: Starbeck's wife, "a rosy matron with puffy, slack features." After a humiliatingly intercepted and exposed trick, Vogler proceeds to a vicious mesmeric exposure of the foibles and unappetizing family life of the Starbecks, ruthlessly using Mrs. Starbeck as his instrument. Then follows "The Invisible Chain" number, using Antonsson as dupe. Lashed to fury by the trick that holds him powerless, Antonsson lunges at Vogler the instant he is freed from the spell and throttles the magician, who falls motionless to the floor. Vergérus pronounces the magician dead, arranges for an autopsy, and has the body transferred to the attic in the black casket.

Now follows a bizarre kaleidoscope of reactions: everyone tries to be nice to Manda, who remains unmoved and quiet; Sofia finally firmly carries Tubal off to save his soul in her bedroom and to make an end of his swindling days, now that he will settle down as a good Christian and marry her; Vergérus and Starbeck in the little attic prepare a covering story to explain the events of the last twelve hours; Starbeck departs and Vergérus returns to the attic; on his way out Starbeck has a snarling little interlude with Granny, who pads out to the laundry room, peeks in, and then climbs up on a barrel to cut down the hanging body of the suicide Antonsson; Egerman submits to his wife's bitter reproaches for allowing this terrible thing to happen to Vogler out of mere desire for revenge.

The scene shifts to the attic, where Vergérus is writing. Suddenly "another hand lays itself quietly over his left hand." Thus begins the hideous nightmare sequence that drives the royal counselor on medicine to the verge of insanity from sheer terror. For Vogler seems to have come alive again. After a horrifying pursuit around the little attic and down the stairs, Vergérus is saved at the last moment by Manda, who appears and commands her husband to leave Vergérus alone. We learn in a brief sharp interchange that the dead man dissected in the autopsy was none other than the poor actor Spegel, with whom Vogler "changed places on the floor in the hall" after the supposedly fatal attack by Antonsson and in the flurry consequent upon that attack.

Vergérus, for fairly obvious reasons, now promises Vogler to help him square things with the police and the authorities in Stockholm. But the magician's troupe is in the process of dissolution. Tubal has found his Sofia (or vice versa), and Granny announces that she has hoarded enough money to quit this disreputable life and open a little "apothecary for specialties." Sara decides at the last moment to come along with the Voglers since she wants more of her "little Simson."

Amid this confusion an almost crazed Starbeck rushes back into the Egerman house bearing a command from the king that Vogler shall appear before him for a royal performance. Understandably relieved that he will still be able, after all, to produce the magician, he ceremoniously and obsequiously ushers the magician out to his carriage.

The Magician is thus explicitly and professedly an ambivalent, equivocal story about mesmerism, spiritist antics, human foibles ruthlessly exposed, a sleazy if punctilious surface and a vast tumultuous underground that reaches now far beyond the mere subconscious of any human individual or even any group or indeed even of the entire human race. It is patently and palpably a thing of lights and shadows: occult performances are notoriously more convincing when given in broad daylight, and the magician Vogler turns this taunt against his tormenter to give the royal counselor on medicine the fright of his life just before noon in a little attic room; Sofia, the enormous and sexually insatiable cook is a bustling determined figure of the daylight; Sara and Sanna, Rustan and Simson, for all their quirks and foibles, are basically healthy young overgrown children cavort-

61

ing a little clumsily because they have not yet learned the sophistication of sex; the magician himself is left at the end voluntarily in rags and without his stage makeup in the clear light of a July afternoon.

But behind this surface ordinariness lurk and scutter strange apparitions: a dying actor plucked at nightfall from a marshy puddle and driven forward to haunt a bourgeois home; a murderer surprised hanging from a hook in a dark corner of a laundry and cut down by an eerie old woman who has foretold his fate and posture hours before and who almost certainly knows that this suicide is not technically a murderer at all since his victim is still very much alive; that old woman herself furtively snatching up things that look like black stones from holes in the loamy forest; the somber horror of cheap tricks that suddenly precipitate disgusting revelations; and above all that unmentionable presence evoked by the old woman's repeated incantation:

> Wound in the eye, blood in the mouth, fingers gone, neck broken, he calls you down, he calls you forth, beyond the dead, the living, the living dead, beyond the raised hands . . .[1]

The bidimensional light-and-shadow character of *The Magician* is so patently typical of this film as contradistinguished from any other in the series that we must search for the vital clue to its God-dynamic and its exploration of the human situation precisely in terms of that bidimensionality. The exploration of the human situation is effected in the daylight dimension of this film; that is what makes the probing into the depths of lost man's heart so peculiarly hideous and appalling. The entire God-dynamic, the whole probing into the God-man relationship and the Luciferian thrust of Vogler plays itself out in the night dimension, the shadowy darkness.

The two dimensions intermingle as they will again to an even greater degree in *Through a Glass Darkly*. But in *The Magician* they intermingle necromantically, by incantation, spell, magic, charms, and even tricks. It is in this peculiar sort of intermingling that the key to the place of this film in the dynamic of the series must be sought. Man has no meaningful contact with God, said *The Seventh Seal*; man is loveless, said *Wild Strawberries*; out of his lovelessness man makes contact with dark powers, says *The Magician*.

The depth probe of man, though considerably complicated by subplots, is tolerably simple and straightforward, even though there clings to its edges that chilling equivocation so typical of the entire film. The God-probing is subtler, more episodic and secretively scrabbling, compounded of the scutter of little rat feet of fear and the lurid revelations of sudden lightning flashes cleaving a beneficent dark that masks nameless horrors. Of absolutely capital significance to an understanding of the God-dynamic of this film is the old woman's incantation already reported: for when we shall have penetrated the exact identity of the presence so summoned, we shall have broken the code of the God-dimension of this most frightening film of our entire series. Preceding films have been somber or nostalgically disturbing; succeeding films will be heartbreaking, gripping, suffocating, or overwhelming. *The Magician* alone is starkly and uncompromisingly *frightening*: a power has got loose in the volcanic upheaval that is the syndrome of modern man, and dark things are being perpetrated by loveless hearts, shallow minds, and hate-filled souls; but also, but more terrifying still, by more than human presences, ultimately by one disastrous presence, the paradigm of the end result of the rebellious upheaval, the ravaged cadaver of the hanged man, *the crucified God!*

Death is endemic to this film, as we shall see; love is present too as a deformed and blowsy procession of lustful spasms, as a torment, a sadness, a fragile and equivocal hope and goad. And God creeps through *The Magician* almost entirely deformed. His silence, bitterly lamented in *The Seventh Seal* ("I call out to him in the dark but no one seems to be there") and nostalgically but equably regretted in *Wild Strawberries* ("Where is the friend I seek everywhere? Dawn is the time of loneliness and care"), is savagely pilloried in *The Magician* by a skeptical royal counselor on medicine as productive of cheap occultism and theologizing alike:

> But miracles don't happen. It's always the apparatus and the spiel which have to do the work. The clergy have the same sad experience. God is silent and people chatter.[2]

Now this same royal counselor on medicine is curious about the magician's claims and determined to expose him; and this for a very interesting reason, which indicates a slight circularity in the argument the counselor advances above:

VERGERUS: Indeed, Mrs. Egerman. Your husband holds the opinion that intangible and inexplicable forces really exist.
OTTILIA: And you deny that possibility.
VERGERUS: It would be a catastrophe if scientists were suddenly forced to accept the inexplicable.
EGERMAN: Why a catastrophe?
VERGERUS: It would lead to the point where we would have to take into account a . . . that we would be suddenly forced to . . . logically we would have to conceive of . . .
EGERMAN: A God.
VERGERUS: A God, if you like.
STARBECK: A grotesque thought, and besides it's not modern. . . .[3]

Spegel, the decrepit actor, is the arrow pointing from the daytime dimension to the nightside of this film's universe. In a manner of speaking (and one is never allowed to be unequivocally certain where the ultimate truth or the ultimate reality lies), Spegel crosses over into death and returns. Then, in a strange substitutional death (which of course must not be pushed too far), Spegel enters the dark kingdom definitively so that Vogler may escape it. There is a deal of trickery throughout in this regard and a horrifying fortuitousness about the "murder" willed but not accomplished technically.

In the same way, death in *The Magician* takes on an especially horrible cast. Death is here no longer simply the black-robed objective figure beckoning man to a somber transformation, incomparably more than the mere hopeless finality that rings the universe of man in *Wild Strawberries*. Death here is crept into the very vitals of man, not as a comforting if intransigent terminal reality but as the doorway to something namelessly malignant and horrifying.

Spegel analyzes the anatomy of his own death for Vogler:

> If you want to register the moment itself, look closely, sir. I'll keep my face open to your curiosity. What do I feel? Fear and well-being. Now death has reached my hands, my arms, my feet, my bowels. It climbs upward, inward. Observe me closely. Now the heart stops, now my consciousness becomes extinguished. I see neither God nor angels. I am dead. You wonder. I will tell you. Death is . . .[4]

That is bad enough but still reminiscent of nothing worse than a sort of actualization in real waking life of Isak Borg's awful dream. But the "returned" Spegel has incomparably more disturbing things to say:

> I am already in a state of decomposition. . . . One walks step by step into the darkness. The motion itself is the only truth. . . . When I thought I was dead, I was tormented by horrible dreams.[5]

The key here is decomposition. The dead in *Wild Strawberries* rest easy and dreamlessly after the fruit that was their little modest life has been spilled; and the living who dream nightmares meet their horror only in the notion of the passive immobility of death which puts period even to dreaming. But the dead in *The Magician* do not rest easy; they prowl the night. And the living burghers are not simply dead though still alive, like old Isak; rather these burghers have entered that nauseating stage of decomposition, evoked by Mrs. Starbeck's persistent references to stomach gases, by Mrs. Egerman's swollen face, by the repeated picture of the hanged man, and most horribly by the nauseous presence of the nameless horror that is the object of the old woman's incantation.

Death is not simply the wearing out of a mechanism, the running down of a spring. Death here is a violent event: murder, hanging, and the reek of sin are its context. The old woman lashes out in furious mockery of Tubal's whistling-in-the-dark "explanation" of the wailing cry the wayfarers hear in the forest:

GRANDMOTHER   *(mimics him):* It's a fox! A fox on two wasted legs, bloody, with his head hanging by a few sinews perhaps. A fox without eyes, but with a rotten hole for a mouth . . . I have seen them, I have. And I know what I know.[6]

And out of all the equivocal trickery of the fateful hours spent by the Vogler troupe in Egerman's house, one absolutely solid fact emerges: the corpse of the coachman who wanted to be a murderer, thought he was a murderer, and so hanged himself in the laundry. Human power untethered by a mighty love turned destructive, first of others and finally of itself.

As clearly as a warning bell, the message sounds forth from *The Magician* that the restrictive humanistic world of *Wild Strawberries* is not and cannot be fireproof and hermetically self-contained, even in its apparently straightforward hopelessness. Man was not built to live without hope; and if the true hope is killed, then dream hopes and finally very quickly nightmare hopes will leap up in its stead. Vogler has crossed a far more fateful line than he imagines; he thinks he has lost his faith in supernatural healing power, but in reality he has abandoned his openhearted trust in a divine healing love, given over to the human heart to render operative in pain and suffering in this fallen world. If the human heart rebels at that heavy assignment, then it can only attempt the death and destruction of others, ultimately of the very source of that love, God himself. And when Vogler succumbs to the temptation to use his power for an easy conquest of money and prestige, he begins to become a destroyer.

Tubal's phraseology is of course unctuous and equivocal, but his message is supremely relevant to the Vogler syndrome. For Tubal tells young Sara:

66

Little child, let us not speak of supernatural things. Let us instead enjoy reality, which is considerably more natural, not to say more wholesome. That which is secret, that which is hidden, the ghosts of the dead, the vision of the future which hangs over us with its threatening dark face, all this we ought to leave be, my child.[7]

The knight has begged for guarantees, old Isak has begged for grace, and the icy skeptic of this film incisively articulates the same demand of the pusillanimous human heart in a strange little interchange with Manda:

MANDA: If just once . . .
VERGÉRUS: That's what they all say. If just once. For the faithless, but above all for the faithful. If just once.
MANDA: If just once—that's true.[8]

All these have demanded a sign and there shall no sign be given them, save the sign of Jonas who was in the whale's belly for three days! In the dark cavern of visceral human confusion, abandoned deliberately by a Lover-God determined to allow their freedom to function, mortals must hack out peace and love and beauty and goodness with no tools save their frantically upward-beating open human hearts.

Spegel has had a glimmering of this insight, for he cries out in Vogler's carriage:

I have always yearned for a knife. A blade with which to lay bare my bowels. To detach my brain, my heart. To free me from my substance. To cut away my tongue and my manhood. A sharp knife blade which would scrape out all my uncleanliness. Then the so-called spirit could ascend out of this meaningless carcass.[9]

The desire that seems to be a humble justification is in reality the epitome of cowardly evasion. For man is not meant to be used or handled or wielded as a passive tool by any mechanistically omnipotent God. He is assigned to the stimulating and appalling task of the glory and the terror of created freedom. And he must ultimately take up that challenge like a free man, in humility and openness to be sure, but also in courage and fortitude. Otherwise he can only end by actively crucifying God.

The mortal who will not walk on the dark path of freedom, of the free adventurous human response to the perfect love of God the Free, must inevitably become a malefactor, trying to purchase with counterfeit coin what can only be conquested by the true coin of God's realm, the free agony of the righteous heart. So it is that love, in the universe of *The Magician*, has sunk far below the level even of the shallow egotistical humanism of Borg's comfortable world. Love has now become something to be purchased by magic, by love potions.

In such a universe of necromantic power seekers and love buyers, what can happen to God? He must shrivel to the status of a witch, for in such a universe the tattered diseased remnants of religious faith will worship only occult power. Yet the transcendent Lover-God will take his own way through this nightmare, and the distortion of his features will fail entirely to touch his substance. The creeping surreptitious figure of Granny, who slinks along the nightside of this film, gradually reveals the God-drama here in process, until the macabre and yet oddly haunting moment when she flashes forth for a few moments the true face of God as she sings a love song to a frightened girl.

At the outset of the film she is shown scrabbling in the earth for something hidden there:

> She kneels and searches in the hole with her hand, looks rather satisfied, fishes up something which can best be described as a black stone. She looks carefully over her shoulder to see if the others are watching, but when no one seems to be taking notice she puts her find in a small leather bag she carries.[10]

At the end she reveals to her grandson what she has been up to:

> You look at my bags and then perhaps you wonder? Very well, look. It's six thousand riksdalers which Granny has collected over the years and buried here and there. . . . I'm going to buy respectability with it. (Whispers) An apothecary, for example. (Whispers) An apothecary for specialties.[11]

And she scornfully informs Vogler that their ways henceforth shall lie apart, that she will walk no more with him and his ridiculous troupe of fakers.

Tubal almost verbally identifies the presence behind the mask of Grandmother and simultaneously pinpoints an important strand of modern agnosticism, deliberate agnosticism, contributing to God's silence:

> Granny's tricks are passé. They're no fun any more because they can't be explained. Granny, you ought to be dead.[12]

Granny herself tells the frightened young Sanna:

> Nowadays nobody believes in my secrets, so I have to be careful. One must not offend the new faith, because then one might be put in a madhouse.[13]

This God is deliberately neglected and reviled and spurned and derided because modern man wants to have complete control of his own destiny with the added security of a mechanistic, necromantic capacity to push that destiny to infallible and automatic happiness, bypassing entirely the dark road of open daring love. God therefore keeps cannily silent and stores up his riksdalers, his royal coin to purchase respectability in the form of an apothecary where he may perhaps one day dispense a "medicine for mortality."

And in this darkest moment of the God-dynamic to be encountered in any of the films, the old witch gives a young girl a present and sings her a song, before slipping out to an abominable rendezvous.

Sanna is the only one in that ill-fated house of Egerman who does not enter at all into the love-buying spree that catches up the redoubtable Sofia, the ingenuously lustful young Sara, the gangling Rustan, the pathetic Mrs. Egerman. Sanna is frightened throughout and holds back. Now Grandmother tells her:

> Hush, hush. You shouldn't be sad, little ant. You'll soon be in the game. First Grandmother gives you a gift to console you.

Hush, hush. Now I'll sit here and sing to you so that you'll fall asleep.[14]

The gift and the song are a positive declamation of God's purpose for man, a manifesto of God the Free All-Powerful Lover against the ridiculous posturings of man the necromantic destructive egotist. And gift and song taken together point ineluctably to that awful rendezvous for which old Granny has so long been somewhat apprehensively waiting.

The gift is a reminder, a not too arcane hint, that man is indeed not alone; the song is a trenchant explication of what God aims at in this strange act of creating a being who can love and who is free.

The gift is an ear:

And if you whisper your wishes into this ear, you'll get what you ask for. But only on one condition. . . . You can only ask for things that live, are living, or can become alive.[15]

The song is of a soldier who fights bravely against an enemy army while murmuring without ceasing the name of his bride. When the battle has been won, the soldier writes "a letter of love to his bride":

I felt your thoughts of me through the strife;
It is this which surely spared my life.
And now I stand on watch this night,
Knowing that your love has heavenly might.

And Granny adds a still more explicit envoi:

Love is trust and love is rest,
Love gives strength to the cowardly breast;
Love is one and never two,
Love is for every lover new.[16]

This is the love that renews the fact of the earth; this is the true destiny of free man. Neither to cower in the dandling embrace of a smothering omnipotence allied to paternalistic overprotectiveness nor yet to strike out in rebellious autonomy to make his own fortune and save himself; but rather to fight gal-

lantly at the barricades while murmuring the name of the beloved who can only wait at home and watch the battle because
that beloved wills that the human lover shall win the spurs of
his freedom.

But what if the human lover in fact falters? What if he rebels?
Then the drama must proceed, for God will not abdicate his
adventure of freedom, knowing full well in his inscrutable wisdom that this freedom, this free man, is worth all the tears of
the world, worth even Calvary, which is rapidly approaching.
For though theologians who speak in the restricted vocabulary
of discursive human rationality must choose their words with
contradistinguishing care, the Christian poet can fearlessly aver
that with the first human murder Calvary was not only rendered
inevitable but in fact begun. If man rebels and falters, then pain
and death and murder will follow, and ultimately deicide. For
we are not here involved in a geometrical theological ratiocina-
tion but in a personal living drama. Rebellious man's freedom
can be respected only in two ways, radically speaking: either
God must abandon him to his fate (and this alternative is precisely articulated in Granny's later separation in the flesh from
Vogler and all his business) or else God must descend and enter
into the pain and murder and horror, to be with his murderer-
creature as a murderee and restorer.

And this latter alternative is the one so plastically mimed
by this God-mouthpiece in this horror film:

> Grandmother listens tensely for something else, something
> which had sounded frightening in the stillness.
> She patters noiselessly out into the large hallway. The door to
> the courtyard stands ajar, but the lamp over the portal has gone
> out. She stands, a small figure in the grayish light, listening
> tensely. Now there is a soundless flash; Grandmother waits, im-
> mobile and expectant. She hears a moaning nearby, a few shuf-
> fling footsteps and then silence again.

> GRANDMOTHER (mumbles): "He calls you down, he calls you out,
> beyond the dead, the living, the living dead, be-
> yond the raised hands." [17]

The moan is, of course, that of the revived Spegel who is prowling the courtyard and is shortly to give Antonsson and Rustan the fright of their lives. In the laundry, so soon to receive Antonsson's despairing corpse, Sara and Simson are locked in panting amorous embrace. Upstairs the pathetic Ottilia Egerman is preparing to greet as a savior the magician who is about to play the cruelest of his destructive tricks. Vergérus is on the point of commencing the dialogue on miracles with Manda Vogler. But it is in Granny's corner that the climax of the God-dynamic is being attained:

> *She moistens her finger, scribbles a sign on the wall and starts upstairs, a gray shadow without substance in the immobile gray light.*[18]

It cannot escape our attention that the magician Vogler is silent, at least in public, until almost the end of the film, feigning to be a mute. But this silence is not the silence of God; it is the protective carapace of the hate-filled misanthrope, the quack trappings of the dubious necromancer. There is another silence, framed by that soundless flash in the grayish light. Granny scribbles a sign on the wall, probably consciously intending to ward off malign spirits and the prowling undead; but she scribbles better than she knows, in the poetic dimension of this God-dynamic.

It is of utmost importance here to recall again that no individual sign or orientation pointer must be pushed too far, on pain of subverting a subtle dramatic dynamic into a bumptious tenth-rate miracle play, unconvincing and self-contradictory to boot. Granny, like Death and Isak's mother, is but a mouthpiece; like every prophet she mixes much that is human, fallible, and even reprehensible with the dreadful message she brings from "beyond the dead, the living, the living dead." Her words and deeds are partly her own; and her revelations are likewise fragmentary and partial. Not until we reach the final film do we encounter in Elizabeth Vogler a total theophany; and there, significantly enough, the protagonist never speaks— she only *is*.

Granny is a somewhat addled, shrewish-tongued old medicine woman. Yet in the gray light she points imperiously to an ultimate and horrifying strand of the God-dynamic. Her spell or incantation is not her own invention; it is some piece of ancient forgotten lore she mouths again and again. The hanged man, a dead man walking, "I have known several hangmen, especially in past years," "the dead, the living, the living dead," the substantial death of Spegel the actor in place of Vogler the guilty schemer—to what rendezvous of heaven and hell do all these arrows point, in the dimension of poetic imagination? But precisely because we are moving through a genuine existential drama rather than a faded devotional representation, the gallows of God are not ringed with any pious halo of religious propriety and Granny can indeed croak:

> One sees what one sees and one knows what one knows. It doesn't smell good in here. Today smells sour, but tomorrow smells rotten, and then it's best to withdraw. . . . Well, someone will be killed, maybe you, maybe me.[19]

The bidimensionality of *The Magician* (surface and depths, dayside of this worldly reality and nightside of preternatural phenomena) is its substantive stage setting, and there is a perpetual disturbing fluid passage from one to the other. *The Magician* writes finis to all hopes of the self-contained finiteness of the Borgian world of restrictive humanism and proclaims the uneasy coexistence of two realms. It is by no means certain yet that the hidden realm contains any radiant healing beauty; indeed exactly the opposite seems rather to be the threatening case. But it is already clear that Bergman is persuaded that the two realms must interact, must implode on each other. The next film, *Through a Glass Darkly*, will picture that mutual implosion. It will be the last film of the series in which the specifically preternatural will play a part. Thereafter we shall have penetrated into the supremely awesome dimension in which plain simple facts emerge as more monstrous and more thrilling than any specters behind the wallpaper. Of *The Magician* it must be said, in Tubal's fulsome yet incisively accurate terms, "the strange powers of Mr. Vogler and his assistant give even more tangible proof of the diabolical aspects of our world order." [20]

As far as I am aware, the devil never emerges in any Bergman film as a radical personal principle of evil; always Bergman's focus of interest is man himself, and preeminently man as seeker and defiant rebel liege of God. But Satan is there in the background; and man's challenging misuse of his own powers of freedom, man's twisted course of short-circuiting seeking for certainty, comfort, and power, is always palpably manifested as a kind of dayside epiphenomenon of the nightside horror of "the diabolical aspects of our world order."

Nor does the question of man's own credence trouble Bergman the creative and evocative artist. His attitude parallels that of the venerable Bishop Bodelschwingh, of whom it is reported that he queried a brash young incipient National Socialist in the Germany of the early thirties as to the youngster's opinion of diabolical powers. The boy haughtily retorted, "We are much too sophisticated these days to believe in devils!"

"What?" countered Bodelschwingh, "You do not believe in them; but then you are utterly and entirely exposed to them and at their mercy."

Specifically, in the context of *The Magician*, we should advert to the revival of necromancy these days under a thousand guises, from horoscopes to Black Masses, from the dubious brand of "parapsychology" to voodoo and the crowded mental hospitals of our day (for many mentally ill persons themselves tell harrowing tales of "possession" and weird preternatural experiences). This revival of interest in and apparent experience of the necromantic should not be too hastily interpreted as the dark side of a religious phenomenon: it may simply witness to a mental instability within a perfectly acceptable atheistic naturalistic context. But it does indicate that something quite specific is wrong within the soul of modern man. It certainly suggests that there are voices in man's blood that cannot easily be stilled, and that when miracle is removed, magic may well strive to take its place. It suggests that, even though there be no God, man still desires to get possession of him and his power. But magicians are dangerous at best and heartless at worst. And the thrust into those dark powers seems ineluctibly to lead to a truly hellish rendezvous, as signaled by old Granny.

EVADING

Through a Glass Darkly

The God who came out was a spider.

David, a middle-aged widower and somewhat lurid though pretentious novelist, has just returned from a creative jaunt in Switzerland to his Scandinavian house on the long shady promontory. As he and his son-in-law, Martin, lay out the nets, Martin asks if David has received the letter he wrote about Karin, David's daughter and Martin's unhappy and already dangerously neurotic wife. David has not received any letter. Karin herself is fetching the milk with her adolescent brother, Minus; they chatter about their father's amatory involvement, apparently now ended, with a shadowy Marianne. Minus remarks that his father's great desire is to be regarded as a literary genius. Karin teases Minus about his lanky stature and lack of a girlfriend. Thunder rumbles in the evening distance and Karin expresses her fear of something nameless. Martin and David continue their discussion about Karin: she returned only a month ago from the hospital; she is restless at nights and her hearing is oversensitive; Martin is helpless before his young wife's progressing illness and David has been so busy with his novel that Martin has hesitated to bother him with the problem. Karin and Minus continue their discussion of lovemaking and women generally: Minus is revealed as a mixed-up, touchy teenager, but his genuine if bemused affection for his sister is obvious.

Brother and sister perform a little play for their father in honor of his return. It does not quite come off, and the oddly assorted quartet retire uneasily for the night. Karin and Martin try unsuccessfully to discuss her illness; a sleepless and disturbed Minus tries equally unsuccessfully to chat with his father.

Just before sunrise Karin leaves her husband's bed and goes to an empty room of the house where she has been hearing things behind the wallpaper. After a strange and dubious experience in this room, she seeks out her father, David, who is polishing his novel: another unsuccessful attempt at communication, until Karin, exhausted, falls asleep and David goes off with Minus to bring up the nets. Karin, waking, finds in her father's desk a notebook with an entry to the effect that her illness is hopeless and that her father is horrified to find himself following its course with simple curiosity. She wanders back to her husband to wake him so that they may go for a swim. She tells him what she has found in her father's notebook; Martin insists that David simply misunderstood his warning that Karin might have a relapse.

Later Karin and Minus, left alone together, again begin a desultory teasing dialogue, swiftly changing into Karin's revelation of her strange clairaudient experiences; she takes her young brother to the room, tells him she is already a sort of wanderer between the two worlds: the world behind the wallpaper, where roam strange beings waiting for God to reveal himself; and the world of the little Scandinavian house with its four inhabitants so curiously unable to communicate. She pledges young Minus to utter secrecy about all this.

David and Martin pursue their talk about Karin: Martin accuses David of total callousness; David responds by telling about his unsuccessful suicide attempt in Switzerland. The aftermath of this grim attempt, prompted by David's sense of utter emptiness and despair about himself as novelist and as father, indeed as human being, has been a birth in himself of a tremulous love for Karin, Minus, and even Martin. David and Martin push off in their boat on their shopping trip into town.

Rain is in the air and seabirds are screeching as Minus and Karin sit on the old jetty. Karin suddenly vanishes, announcing that the rain is upon them, though Minus can only see the gray silent sea. Minus races to the house, to the wallpaper room, searches desperately for his sister, finds her nowhere in the house, races back to the jetty, and finally discovers her crouching in the hull of an old rotten boat. The scenario is eloquent: "Suddenly she has clasped him tight and he falls headlong on top of her, struggles to get free, but can't, sinks more deeply into her. He catches a glimpse of naked skin, an odour of seaweed, rotten wood, the sea bottom. She holds him tight to her with her arms and legs, but her face is averted, her mouth tightly closed." After this shattering experience poor Minus tries to persuade Karin to come to the house but she says she is ill and cannot. He races back to get blankets, mutters a feverish and desperate prayer, and returns again to the rotting old boat. There Martin and David find the two youngsters later and carry Karin back to the house, where she almost immediately agrees to return to the hospital. Before the ambulance plane can arrive, Karin has experienced another and supreme clairaudient experience which this time merges into a clairvoyant experience as well: as she tells her horrified husband, father, and brother, she has seen God and God was a spider.

Karin is taken away to hospital, and Minus and David begin for the first time a really successful and meaningful conversation about love—and God.

The scalpel of the creative artist is probing deeper and deeper; and the human wayfarer and pilgrim is being driven closer and closer to the terrible rendezvous with his own free created self and his free Creator. Man has no meaningful contact with God, said *The Seventh Seal;* man is loveless, said *Wild Strawberries;* out of his lovelessness man makes contact with dark powers, said *The Magician;* the darkest of these powers surge up from man's own inmost heart and issue in sterile narcissistic tragedy, says *Through a Glass Darkly.*

For the most significant key to the understanding of the God-and-man dynamic of this film lies in the realization that Karin, abandoned and misunderstood as she certainly has been by her fellow mortals, yet contributes to her own tragedy and involves her unfortunate brother in it. Karin is a seeker, to be sure, but she is an utterly passive seeker; therein lies the root of her tragedy, for the utterly passive seeker unwilling to contribute anything personal except mere receptivity can only arrive at a theophany that is a sterile narcissistic spider.

Through a Glass Darkly probes the mutual implosion of the this-worldly dimension and another dimension. This mutual implosion is palpably and plastically articulated by the strange device of Karin's experience with the thing behind the wallpaper. The girl is the daughter of a basically narcissistic novel-writing father whose son-in-law bitterly reproaches him:

> In your emptiness there's no room for feelings, and as for any sense of decency, you just haven't got it. You know how everything should be expressed. At every moment you have the right word. There's only *one* phenomenon you haven't an inkling of: life itself. . . . You're cowardly and sloppy, but on one point you're almost a genius. At explaining things away and apologizing.[1]

But this same trenchant and perceptive critic of Karin's father, this fairly competent surgeon and utterly ineffectual husband, Martin, understands poor Karin quite as little as does her father. Karin lashes out at Martin:

> That's the odd thing about you. You always say the right words and do exactly the right things. But they're wrong, even so. . . .

> Anyone who really loves always does the right thing by the person he loves.[2]

In fact both Karin's father and her husband are seeing her only through a glass darkly, through the glass of their own highly narcissistic preoccupations, the husband with his love for this girl as one *he cherishes* rather than as a free unique human partner, the father with his own artistic ambitions which have made him neglect both his now-dead wife and his still-living but desperately endangered daughter.

And this tormented girl, already under treatment for extreme nervous disorders, begins to discover that she can hear another world moving behind the wallpaper of one dreadful and ominous little room in that bourgeois house. From the comfortless bed she shares with her decent but ineffectual husband, Karin pads out one morning just before sunrise into this awful room. The very length and precision of Bergman's description alerts us to the capital significance of the symbolism, articulating in a stacatto series of almost physically painful visual impressions the dangerous sagging of this bourgeois world and the insistent thrust toward a breakthrough on the part of another dubious and drastically different dimension:

> *Karin hesitates, but then goes into the room which looks out toward the sunrise. She tries to close the door behind her but the frame has warped and the lock is broken.*
>
> *Apart from an old Windsor chair and a little nursery table, this room is void of furniture. The floor, which once consisted of clean-scrubbed boards, has been partially ripped up and the floorboards are propped against the wall. What immediately strikes the eye in this room, however, is its wallpaper. Green in colour, it is really supposed to represent leaves in various shades, tones and tinges. In some spots the colour has faded completely and the pattern appears only very faint and grey; but in the corners and behind the pictures the foliage is still strong and leafy. In the wall to the right of the window is a narrow door, also covered with wallpaper, above which a patch of damp has exploded and given birth to a laughing moon-face with one dud eye, a gaping mouth and a huge potato nose. To the left of the window, over the whole*

width of one strip, the pattern of leaves has been ripped away, and behind it a stiff brownish composition with fading golden edges has come into view.

Karin has come to a halt in the middle of the room; her posture is one of petrified attentiveness, as if expecting to hear someone speak to her. She has let go of her dressing-gown and holds her hand out motionlessly before her; her head is turned to one side and her gaze is fixed on the right-hand wall.

Suddenly, small flames of fire are alight in the heavy petals of the wallpaper, a convulsive puff of wind comes from the sea and the house sighs like an old ship with its masts and rigging.

The disc of the sun comes rolling out of the grey ocean swell and little orange tongues of fire flicker over the wallpaper's leafy designs.

Karin gives a sigh, breathes deeply; a sound, as of repressed singing or whispering, stirs in her throat. Her face swells and darkens and her eyes become glazed, unaware.

Slowly she sinks down on her knees, legs wide apart.[3]

This posture and a still more equivocal (or unequivocal!) one in which poor Minus observes Karin in this same room [4] are a clear warning that this unfortunate muddled girl is slipping rapidly into a pseudomystical dream world with strong overtones of introverted sexual narcissism. She has been desperately searching for love without any rudder to guide her. Sickened and dissatisfied with the shallow bourgeois world of her reality, she has opened herself to any love source that may be prowling and is meanwhile surreptitiously seeking at least an assuagement of her longing at her own hands. The stage is already set for the incestuous tragedy. For young Minus, himself a highly confused youngster, is the only real human being who offers Karin any sympathy at all.

Karin tries to tell Martin, her husband, at least a little about her horrible experiences and the torturing split that is opening in her soul:

Sometimes one is so defenceless. . . . Like children exposed in the desert at night. The owls come flying by and look at you out

of their yellow eyes. There are paddings and rustlings and soughings and sighings. And all the damp noses nosing. And wolves'
teeth.[5]

With the more sympathetic Minus she finds she can be much
more explicit:

> Early this morning I was woken by a voice calling me, quite
> definitely calling. I got up and came to this room. Just at sunrise,
> and inside me a tremendous longing, a tremendous power. One
> day someone called to me from behind the wallpaper, and I
> looked inside the cupboard, but it was empty. The voice went on
> calling me, so I pressed myself against the wall and it opened up
> like a lot of leaves *and there I was inside!* [6]

With the incisive precision of detail of the neurally disturbed,
Karin identifies the central nucleus of the other world into which
she has stepped:

> I come into a big room, quite still and silent, people are moving
> about and someone speaks to me and I understand. It's so lovely,
> I feel so safe. Some of the faces are radiant with light.
> All are waiting for him who is to come, but no one worries.
> They say I can be with them when it happens. . . . I long for that
> moment when the door will open and all faces are turned toward
> him who's to come. . . . no one has said anything definite, but I
> believe God is going to reveal himself to us. And he'll come in to
> us through that door. *(Pause)* Everyone's so calm—and so gentle.
> And they're waiting. And their love . . . LOVE . . .[7]

It will be useful at once to pursue this strand of the alleged
God-expectation and God-revelation in Karin's other world to its
bitter and disastrous (and blasphemous and worse than atheistic) conclusion. For there is real pith in the allegation, maintained
by some with whom I have spoken, that this film is a definitive
antitheistic manifesto, furiously proclaiming that the God-notion
is the spawn of a diseased mind and can issue only in despair
and madness, or worse still that the deity, if a deity exists, is
utterly and abominably ahuman and malign. There is pith in
such an allegation only, however, if this one strand of this film

is taken in total abstraction and divorced from the other equally palpably present and poignant strands. Even as Karin seeks an unlovely God in the dimension behind the wallpaper, a heart-rendingly tender strand of his loving mercy is being revealed to her and to us by the gallant efforts of the pitiable young Minus.

In the case of Minus it is especially imperative to remember the warning against any distorting overextension of symbols and to bear always in mind that Bergman is a creative artist making use of that artist's freedom of movement and operating according to that artist's peculiar rhythm of fluid association of disparate symbols and simultaneous multidimensional dynamic of dramatic evolution. The bugbear of all interpretations of parables lies in the pernicious mathematicizing tendency to interpret them exhaustively and to try to find a one-to-one correspondence between every strand of the human story and the transcendent dimension of God. The result is balderdash, sacrilege, and blasphemy, and all the wasted ink, spilled out in an effort to prove that, though he may appear to do so, God does not *really* approve of the unjust steward, the prototype of the Bobby Bakers of this world!

Minus is like God in only two senses: he, as distinct from every other character in this film, is a taut and vibrant energy; and he, as distinct from the two reflective contemplatives and the one tormented mystic, *really acts.* He is unlike God precisely because he is a Swedish adolescent whose action, though prompted by love, is woefully inadequate, whose end effect, though aiming desperately athwart his own confusion at protective tenderness and salvation, is ultimately disintegrative and destructive. Yet Minus is a prophet in his own way, even as Granny was in hers. Something absolutely vital in the God character and in the God-man relationship and its dynamic flashes forth from Minus' distracted strivings. *Caveant theologi!* Let the traditional theologians beware, for Bergman is no quasi-rationalistic expounder of theological geometry; let the New Theologians beware, for Bergman is no revolutionary iconoclast bent on catharsis by way of scandal. He is quite simply a creative theoaesthetic poet.

Karin, then, aims at a mystical vision and ends up in a sanatorium. She scrabbles after her own sort of certitude and clarity of vision, athwart all the terrors and night fears, all the inexplicable gropings of mankind. She is heavy with all the tears and anguish of the world in the wake of the Fall. At film's end, poor Karin, awaiting the ambulance that will take her to the sanatorium, tells of the issue of her vision:

> The door opened. But the god who came out was a spider. He had six legs and moved very fast across the floor. . . . He came up to me and I saw his face, a loathsome, evil face. And he clambered up onto me and tried to force himself into me. But I protected myself. All the time I saw his eyes. They were cold and calm. When he couldn't force himself into me, he climbed quickly up onto my breast and my face and went on up the wall. . . . I've seen God.[8]

This is the radical explication, the palpable actualization, of one of the basic fears that have haunted the earlier films, as man strove forward to see the face of God, strove forward at a pace and with a thrust that afforded the revealing God no scope to show his true face. Death, who obscurely and trenchantly threatened Antonius Block by summoning him to the dark lands of transformation, here emerges as a lethal spider bent on an abominable lethal intercourse. The neglected mother of Isak Borg here scutters out of her retirement to claim her victim in a spasm of matriarchal cannibalism. The old witch of Vogler's world here rushes out to scoop up a final riksdaler, a lost coin of the realm, a totally utilitarian creature serving only the aggrandizement of its Creator. But all because man is throughout searching for himself and not the Utterly Other; all because man, determined above all measure to attain his own comforting certitude, is deforming the face of God to an extent that becomes almost intolerably evident in the great theophanic final film *Persona* in an implacable series of equivocal scenes featuring Nurse Alma's (man's) report of her own shabby and deformed impressions of the simultaneously visible beauty of the physical features of Elizabeth Vogler (God).

Karin is the quintessence of desperate but still cowardly man, pounding on the walls that separate him from what he fondly imagines will be his heart's desire, his comfort, and his peace; screaming for palpable contact with a God tailored to answer his deepest needs and thus already defamed and demeaned to the status, precisely, of a narcissistic dildo. Karin is screaming to be possessed, to be filled, but without giving anything in return; she and her fellow watchers are passively expecting the great ingress of the deity. Well, she gets her wish with a vengeance, and the nightmare of the ingressing spider is but the brackish aftertaste of the awful intercourse in the hull of the rotting boat, where God teaches demanding man the ultimate lesson that an answer by God to man's selfish prayer for a shamanistic divine counterpart can produce only sterile tragedy. Yet, in a mysterious way, within the subtle dynamic of this film God is relaying another message through the tormented Minus; God is willing to try, if only man will respond as free responsible collaborator and not as merely passive sponge.

Almost at the outset of the film Minus and Karin perform the little play for their just returned father. Certainly the play is meant and intended by Minus, its author, to twit the father on his exaggerated devotion to art (i.e., his own fame to be purchased through his novels) and his consequent neglect of his own children. Certainly, in the extremely quicksilver complexity of the artistic cosmos of Bergman, David the father is intended in some sense likewise to be a kind of paradigm of God as seen by men and of man's desperate search for an apparently silent deity. Certainly David effects an ancillary revelation of a mysterious divine dynamic when he tells Martin:

> Out of my emptiness something was born which I hardly dare touch or give a name to. A love. (*Pause*) For Karin and Minus. And you.[9]

Certainly in some sense the line with which Minus ends the film is a theoaesthetic manifesto: "Daddy spoke to me!" [10] And equally certainly, as we shall be seeing, the entire last conversation between the David whose redemption has apparently begun and the frightened Minus represents the supreme evasion which we have designated as the typical contribution of *Through a Glass Darkly to* the God-man dynamic and the silence-of-God problem. Let this suffice to highlight definitively the need for supreme caution and balance in any effort at discursive rationalized interpretations and explication of the successive sunbursts of poetic insight that light the winding path of this film series.

With this caveat, consider the dialogue of that little play performed by brother and sister, consider it in the light of the later awful climax and as pointing toward that climax. In his comic sequences Bergman, like Shakespeare, walks the knife's edge between tears and laughter. Can this buffoonery, whose poignancy emerges only in the retrospect of the dire climax in the rotting old boat, be saved from banality if it be interpreted simply in sociological terms? On the other hand, can anyone sleep undisturbed at night who has allowed, even for a brief moment, its theoaesthetic import to penetrate to his heart and its mysterious consequent theological import to assault his mind?

For Karin as man complains:

> Thereafter he grieved but one hour a day, and now only pays me a courtesy visit on alternate Sundays. His eyes are dry and his thoughts elsewhere.

Minus in the name of God counters:

> Princess, I love you!

Karin as obstreperous man insists:

> I thank you for your kindness. But who are you anyway? Surely you understand I cannot speak to any Tom, Dick or Harry, dead though I may be.

Minus, as modest God, replies:

> Have no fear, sweet lady. In my own kingdom, poor though it is and not large, I am a king. I am an artist.

Karin, as cynical questioning man, throws back:

> An artist?

And Minus delivers a cameo of God:

> In sooth, Princess. I am an artist of purest blood. A poet without poems, a painter without paintings, a musician without music, even an actor without a rôle. The completed work, banal fruit of simple-minded strivings, I despise. My life is my lifework; and it is dedicated to my love for you, Princess.

Karin flings at God the final challenge:

> That sounds beautiful but incredible.

And Minus replies with God's Christian answer:

> I prithee, put me to the proof.[11]

The real-life Karin does indeed put her brother to the proof. Her soggy and desperately demanding passivity articulates the passive scrabbling of medicine-mad man after a pain-killer God, of greedy man after a God little nobler than a vibrator:

> KARIN: You must help me, I'm ill.
> MINUS: Come along, we'll go home.
> KARIN: I can't leave. I must stay here.
> MINUS: What shall we do?
> KARIN: You must help me.
> MINUS: Can't you tell me how to help you?
> KARIN: You must help me.[12]

When all the damage has been done, the pitiable and certainly largely unwitting cause of the whole disaster has found enough glimmering of true love to murmur, "Poor little Minus." [13]

But it is David the father who, out of his newfound humility, yet perpetrates the cardinal evasion of the film. God is despaired of now as an effective healer; but man remains. And David tells his son in effect that man may yet manage to redeem himself. Then will the silence of the highly hypothetical God have been stirred into the lovely sound of happy human singing; man will have given a sort of proof of the possibility of God, the desert will blossom as the rose, and it will be enough. In the ultimate subtle inversion, even man's necessary and mandatory assumption of his own responsibility is here turned upside down by David: for man is hoisting his standard denuded of any heraldry of God, man is shouldering his heavy burden in despair of the everlasting arms underneath him. David's superficially impressive outburst could have been mouthed by any atheistic humanist. It articulates the "certainty achieved" in this film, the certainty to be so implacably unmasked in the succeeding film, *Winter Light.* Bergman, to be sure, does not entirely scorn or pillory the insight of David. But Bergman does insist that this insight is not enough to stand against the roar of the waterfall that is ultimate reality and that will thunder down the gorge of the next film.

This is David's manifesto, the quintessence of humanistic sentimentalized pseudotheology:

> My own hopes lie . . . in the knowledge that love exists as something real in the world of men. . . . *Every* sort of love, Minus! The highest and the lowest, the poorest and the richest, the most ridiculous and the most sublime. The obsessive and the banal. . . . We can't know whether love proves God's existence or whether love is itself God. After all, it doesn't make very much difference. . . . I let my emptiness, my dirty hopelessness, rest in that thought, yes. . . . Suddenly the emptiness turns into wealth, and hopelessness into life. It's like a pardon, Minus. From sentence of death.[14]

Of course, it makes an enormous difference whether love proves God's existence or love is itself God. For the love here referred to is human love. And if it is indeed the ultimate reality, then no higher redemption can be hoped for than the tenuous humanization achieved at the end of this film; whereas if this human loving imperiously points beyond itself to a qualitatively stronger power behind the curtain, then there is hope of a total transformation and healthy rest for man at the end, in the supreme dynamism of the heaven of the redeemed. David's other insight is entirely cogent, the one he articulates in his confession:

> Oh, Karin, how one's eyes burn when one sees oneself. . . . It's like this. One draws a magic circle around oneself, shutting out everything that hasn't any place in one's own private little game. Every time life smashes the circle the game turns into something grey, tiny, ridiculous. So one draws a new circle, builds up new barriers.[15]

But the power that would effectively rend asunder the protective barriers of ultimate personal, national, and ethnic provincialism man builds around himself must be stronger than the humanistic yearning for generosity and communication David himself articulates later on. Otherwise that power will falter even as it does in the face of the demand of the desperate young fisherman Jonas Persson in *Winter Light*, so worried about the Chinese brought up to hate and without love and so soon to come into possession of the bomb!

Young Minus himself could have told his father just how inadequate is the good resolution and even generosity of the human heart, in the absence of the purifying power; and just how trenchantly God refuses to answer our human agonized pleas for strength to solve, on our own terms and within our own dimension, the basic problem that can be resolved only by the transition to the God-dimension across the only sure and safe bridge, openhearted assumption of a lonely and desperate freedom that rests in trembling equilibrium in the greater freedom of God.

For Minus has known the moment of total abandonment as he strove mightily to effect the salvation of his sister who already infected him with her own demanding passivity:

> *Minus rushes into his room and throws himself on his knees on the floor and clasps his hands, bends his head and presses his hands to his lips.*
>
> MINUS *(whispering):*   God . . . God . . . help us!
>
> *Like a cry and a whisper, the rain beats in fierce gusts against the windowpane, blurring all outlines. The room's interior is in semi-darkness and the wind presses against the old house, which sighs and creaks.*
> *Again and again he calls on God. At length, exhausted, he falls silent.*[16]

And Minus has sat in the ruins of human effort at loving and has known that this effort is not enough:

> *Minus is sitting somewhere in eternity with his sick sister in his arms. He is empty, exhausted, frozen. Reality, as he has known it until now, has been shattered, ceased to exist. Neither in his dreams nor his fantasies has he known anything to correspond to this moment of weightlessness and grief. His mind has forced its way through the membrane of merciful ignorance. From this moment on his senses will change and harden, his receptivity will become sharpened, as he goes from the make-believe world of innocence to the torment of insight.*[17]

Minus does indeed tell his father:

> Reality burst and I fell out. It's like in a dream, though real. Anything can happen—*anything*, Daddy! . . . I'm so terrified I could scream.[18]

And it will take more than the superficial (though not utterly worthless or mistaken) humanistic sociological comfort of a David to cope with that terror.

Minus has in fact, doubtless entirely unwittingly, put his finger squarely on the thrilling and profoundly disturbing nucleus of the entire created situation: Anything can happen—anything! There is neither the mechanical certitude of a geometricized predestinational cosmos nor yet the bracing challenge of a completely self-contained humanistic world, ultimately to be probed and organized into a new mechanism by the advances of science and technology. Always in the very center of the stage rages free created man, and always to his encounter comes the supremely free God; and between the two there can only be some species of love-union, but that union can ultimately be only transformation or crucifixion.

When Minus stands entirely revealed as the pathetic Scandinavian adolescent entirely unable to cope with the sickness of his sister or yet to fill her need, God is silent. But this is precisely because he is preparing some better thing than the shabby, though well-meant, incestuous comfort which is the best poor Minus has to offer. And again God is silent precisely because he is insistently demanding that his little children grow up. In one way, of course, Minus' cry for help is far more mature already than the knight's insistence that God stretch forth his hand palpably in the darkness wherein the knight insistently seeks him. For Minus has at least begun to try. But a cozy and relaxing comfort at that crucial moment would have been a total betrayal of God's whole purpose. The crucifix that brooded over the knight's confession and was distant, irrelevant, and musty must brood again over the crisis horror of the pastor in the next film, *Winter Light,* but now it must have become supremely relevant and meaningful. Between the two crucifixes must stand Man the crucified, impaled on the barb of his own insufficiency. For Man is not being summoned to Calvary either to bathe in penitential tears a traditional crucified Pantokrator or to suck up from that cross a mechanically vivifying precious blood. He is being summoned to Calvary for a definitive rendezvous with his own freedom, which he must learn to bear creatively, on pain of effecting another and definitive crucifixion. In pain and terror, Man must learn that "it hath not sufficed"; that he is truly incapable of attaining consummation for himself or for his fellows *within his own dimension*; but that he may not therefore surrender passively to a mechanistically manipulating God, on pain of mere sterility and blasphemous anthropomorphization. And so Minus must be alone, and alone force his way "through the membrane of merciful ignorance"; so that Man may one day stand again before the crucifix and learn how God-Man behaved when he was alone; so that Man, in turn, may address himself to the challenging task of that perpetual self-transcendence that is a perpetual crucifixion; so that, finally, the cosmos may move ahead again on the right path.

What is terrifying about this film is that David has not yet learned the lesson of humanistic insufficiency. With the pathetic and awful example of his own son's pointless and fruitless effort before his eyes, David still presumes to proclaim that his hopes lie "in the knowledge that love exists as something real in the world of men." Love does, of course, so exist, but it is crucified love. What man must learn is that his loving (of fellowman and, above all, of God) must be a steady self-transcendence, never a retrograde involution upon himself or upon his species. Love that is creative does not provide a soporific for the sleepless but rather a stimulant for the wakeful watchers and scouts of the future.

The really crucial problem is that man wants to remain himself and be loved and comforted as such. Yet man's own experience should show him that such stagnation has always been fatal to every biological species before man; why should it be different in man's case? Loaded with the whole weight of the empirical world, with the drag of matter and the restless thrust of mind-spirit, man must stride forward, not merely circle on the pinhead of his present state. Man senses painfully God's silence as a lack of certitude; this lack triggers all manner of efforts by man to attain certitude of some sort by any means other than openhearted surrender and courageous assumption of the responsibility of a free created agent *with an opening onto eternity and transcendence.* And this activism in turn deepens the silence of God by blocking the channels of communication between God and man. Man must learn in pity and terror that God's silence is the silence of a loving free Creator who sets freedom, or more accurately in the existential order, *free creatures,* above all considerations of comfort (their comfort *or his own*). Man must simultaneously learn that the only answer he can be given to his certitude quest is the challenge of the adventure of freedom with its concomitant risks and demands on his own nerve and fortitude.

Through a Glass Darkly is the first of three films that form a closely knit trilogy, and the texts of the three have indeed been published under the title *A Film Trilogy*. It pertains to the very nature of a trilogy that the fundamental subject matter would be common throughout, that the three parts would represent some sort of successive stages of a single dynamic. Bergman's own brief notation and subtitles have confirmed my conviction that in these three films, taken as a dynamic unit, we have reached the heartland of the silence-of-God problematic, *so far as that heartland can be verbally expressed*. One further film will follow, but in it we shall have passed beyond the frontier of verbal expression to the nucleus of mystery, where revelation is visual and a simple theophany. Bergman notes: "The theme of these three films is a 'reduction'—in the metaphysical sense of that word." [19] To the child of the technocratic age, reduction connotes a diminution and a thrust toward the lowest common denominator; to a sound metaphysics, reduction signifies a "leading back" of complexity to fundamental unity and simplicity, of appearances to an ultimate reality, of the derivative to the basic and primordial.

When we now juxtapose the subtitles suggested by Bergman: "certainty achieved" for *Through a Glass Darkly*; "certainty unmasked" for *Winter Light*; and "God's silence—the negative impression" for *The Silence*, we realize that the theme is being centered on certainty and God's silence.

The "certainty achieved" in *Through a Glass Darkly* is the "certainty" that love exists in the world of men and women. The "certainty unmasked" in *Winter Light* (with, as we shall see, a rare direct quotation in the script of one film from the script of its predecessor) is precisely the conviction that this love as such as enough. Conceivably it might be enough for a statically manipulated creation of puppets; it is *not* enough for those to whom has been given the hard and stimulating challenge of transcending. The human "transcender" must look not to himself certainly, not even to the limitless horizons of an empty cosmos around him, but to his Creator; must look to that Creator not for a perfect pattern to be copied with meticulous zeal but rather for a plastic picture of the sort of creative anguish man must take upon himself in the winter light of his hard assignment.

FACING

Winter Light

You must learn to love.

On a gray November Sunday noon, Pastor Tomas Eriksson celebrates the liturgy of the Eucharist in a little church at Mittsunda. He communicates the village school teacher, Märta Lundberg, who is his distracted mistress; the hunchback sexton, Algot Frövik, who suffers cruelly from arthritis; the fear-tormented fisherman, Jonas Persson, and his worried pregnant wife; and an old woman from Hol. These communicants form almost the entire congregation. The organist, Fredrik Blom, strikes up a saccharine final hymn with a real flourish. Pastor Eriksson, influenza-ridden, retreats to the vestry, where solicitous warden Aronsson advises him to get a replacement to take the vespers service that evening at Frostnäs. Tomas says that is impossible; he must go himself. Algot, the sexton, asks to speak to the pastor but is put off until before vespers.

The Perssons sidle into the vestry now, and Mrs. Persson

97

tells the pastor of her husband Jonas' strange worry about the Chinese who are being brought up to hate and soon will have the bomb. Tomas tries a few platitudes. Mrs. Persson nervously insists that Jonas return for a longer chat with the pastor after he has driven her home. As they leave, Märta comes into the vestry, bringing a basket with food and drink. She and Tomas scuffle verbally a little about her persistent desire that he marry her. She leaves him a long letter which he reads while awaiting Persson. This letter is a major theoaesthetic and even theological document, couched in the nervous language of a sniveling but pathetic and even oddly noble and strangely dignified female.

Jonas Persson returns, and Tomas vainly strives to give the young fisherman reasons for going on living despite the Chinese and the bomb. Tomas reveals much of his own feckless and egotistical existence in this interview. Jonas sidles out unconvinced, and Tomas groans with desperation at his conviction that God has somehow abandoned him, him a pastor of the church! He concludes to a liberating atheism and rushes out to the chancel, where he finds Märta. The old woman from Hol comes rushing to tell him Jonas Persson has committed suicide, just down the hill by the torrent.

Tomas and Märta part, as the pastor rushes to the scene of the suicide. He can do nothing; the police are already in charge and the body must be moved to the infirmary for the death certificate. The entire scene is dominated by the deafening roar of the great torrent.

Märta has walked down to join Tomas, and they drive back together to her schoolhouse, where she fetches him some cough mixture and aspirin. While she is gone, Tomas talks to a boy who has come to the school looking for a comic book he had left in his desk. After a violent argument with Märta, in which he reproaches her bitterly with trying to entangle him and being generally petty, Tomas nevertheless consents to invite her to go with him to vespers at Frostnäs.

On the road, as they are stopped for a train crossing, Tomas tells Märta of a terrifying experience he had as a child, when he could not find his father in the house one night after waking in a fright.

Arrived at Frostnäs church, Tomas is approached by Algot for the promised conversation which deals with Christ's abandonment on the cross. Blom, the organist, meanwhile chats oilily with Märta, advising her to get out of the neighborhood while she still can, informing her that Tomas is hopelessly in love with his dead wife, whom Blom describes as a thoroughgoing cheat.

Algot comes to inquire of the pastor whether vespers should begin, now that a reconnaissance has revealed that Märta is the only person in the church apart from Blom. Tomas signals Algot to ring the bell. Märta murmurs a distracted prayer for some sort of reality and genuinity. Tomas comes out of the vestry, goes to the altar, kneels, rises, and turns a pale anxiety-filled face to his congregation. He speaks the last line of the film, surely one of the most arresting of Bergman's many memorable concluding lines: " 'Holy, holy, holy, Lord God Almighty. All the earth is full of his glory . . .' " [1]

Winter Light is the most unequivocally and undeniably religious film of the entire series, a film explicitly dealing with the God-man relationship and with human relationships in terms of that transcendent one.

The desperate search for the all-protecting Father has assumed in *Winter Light* a more lacerating and disturbing consequentiality. It is articulated in a reminiscence of Pastor Tomas as he and his mistress, Märta, are driving in the car to Frostnäs:

> The road turns inland. At the level crossing, just before Frostnäs station, the booms come down, the railway bell clangs and the stop light burns. Tomas brakes and switches off the engine. From far off the train can be heard approaching.

TOMAS: One evening when I was a boy I woke up in a terrible state of fright. The train shrieked down at the corner, you remember we lived in the old vicarage by the bridge.

99

It was an early spring evening with a strange wild light over the ice and the forest. I got out of bed, ran round all the rooms looking for Father. But the house was empty. I shouted and screamed, but no one answered. So I dressed as well as I could and ran down to the shore, all the time screaming and crying for Father.

In a cloud of steam and snow-flurries, the train rolls by with a majestic roar. Its buffers and couplings rattle, and the brakes and axles whine. The carriages lean over and shake as they go round the curve, the points crash and the train comes squealing and panting to a halt at Frostnäs station.

TOMAS: I'd been left without Father and Mother in a completely dead world. I was sick with terror.[2]

In *Winter Light* the accent is clearly on religion, the tragedy of a pastor who can no longer guide his flock because his own faith has wavered, wavered preeminently in function of a disarray in his own personal life, occasioned by his hopeless and necrophiliac devotion to his dead wife; nor is it any accident that this devotion precisely makes him incapable of any meaningful response to the affection offered him by his distracted mistress. Yet, when all is said and done and suffered, Tomas comes to the insight that the one positive contribution he can make is his unequivocal, if fear-ridden, yes to God. Man has no meaningful contact with God, said *The Seventh Seal*; man is loveless, said *Wild Strawberries*; out of his lovelessness man makes contact with dark powers, said *The Magician*; the darkest of these powers surge up from man's own inmost heart and issue in sterile narcissistic tragedy, said *Through a Glass Darkly*; man must break out of this dark circle and can do so only by some drastic affirmation of God, says *Winter Light*.

What is Tomas seeking? He himself provides the not very edifying answer: peace for *his* soul in the cramped little dimensions of that soul: and certainty for *his* mind within the insignificant ambit of that human mentality. To the disturbed fisherman and future suicide, Jonas Persson, the ineffectual Pastor Tomas confesses:

I became a clergyman and believed in God. (*Gives a short laugh*) An improbable, entirely private, fatherly god. Who loved mankind, of course, but most of all me. . . . A god who guaranteed me every imaginable security. Against fear of death. Against fear of life. A god I'd suggested myself into believing in, a god I'd borrowed from various quarters, fabricated with my own hands. D'you understand, Jonas? What a monstrous mistake I'd made? Can you realize what a bad priest must come of such a spoilt, shut-in, anxious wretch as me? [3]

What is Tomas given? The God to whom he can freely cry a few moments after this outburst: "God, my God, why have you abandoned me?" [4] The God of whom a few moments later still he can proclaim: "God does not exist any more. . . . I'm free now. At last, free." [5] The God who can, a few moments later yet, overwhelm him in the thunder of the cataract and the corpse of the suicide, whom Tomas' humanistic vaporings could not restrain from the desperate deed of self-destruction.

How is Tomas seeking the desire of his soul? He himself tells Jonas Persson:

In my darkness and loneliness I hugged him to myself—the only person I showed him to was my wife. She backed me up, encouraged me, helped me, plugged up all the holes. Our dreams. (*He gives a sudden laugh*).[6]

How is Tomas taught he must seek? In the words of the old hunchback sexton at Frostnäs:

To understand that no one has understood you. To be abanboned when one really needs someone to rely on. A terrible suffering. . . . When Christ had been nailed up on the cross and hung there in his torments, he cried out: "God, my God, why hast thou forsaken me?" He cried out as loud as he possibly could. He thought his Father in Heaven had abandoned him. He believed everything he'd been preaching was a lie. The moments before he died, Christ was seized with a great doubt. Surely that must have been his most monstrous suffering of all? I mean God's silence. Isn't that true, Vicar? [7]

By whom is this search being undertaken? By a man of whom and to whom his mistress Märta can truthfully say:

> You're dissatisfied with your life, with everything, most of all with yourself. And here am I, throwing myself into your arms. It doesn't make sense with the rest of the picture.[8]

What manner of man does the searcher become at the end? The man who can still call for the vespers service to begin in Frostnäs chapel, despite the exceedingly small congregation!

Above all, why is Tomas seeking? Actually it is poor Märta, in her sadly muddled humanity, the last of the God-mouthpieces in this series to show such muddled humanity, who provides the answer:

> If only I could lead him out of his emptiness, away from his lie-god. If we could dare to show each other tenderness. If we could believe in a truth . . . If we could believe . . .[9]

In other words, the theological quest of Tomas Eriksson is motivated initially by no higher or other end than a human rescue from human loneliness, a rescue that ends in emptiness.

But thirty seconds later Tomas learns what must be the true *Why?* of his searching. The Bergman scenario is eloquent here:

> *Tomas goes up to the alter, kneels, rises, turns a pale and anxiety-filled face to his congregation:*
>
> TOMAS: "Holy, holy, holy, Lord God Almighty. All the earth is full of his glory . . ."[10]

Tomas Eriksson has been taught that man must seek God not for benefits that this God may confer on man, least of all the dubious benefit of ease and contented-cow comfort, but simply because this God is God and man is his creature. The radiant, austere, celestial love of this God will not shine out until we reach *Persona*, after the awful interposition of the supreme alienation of *The Silence*. For the moment, man must learn in Tomas Eriksson that the only acceptable and redemptive doxology is *Gratias agimus tibi propter magnam gloriam Tuam*—We give thee thanks, not for any good thou mayst will to usward but simply because thou art so beautiful.

And another equally desperate and equally vital lesson man must learn. The humanized pseudo-love is not enough even to cure poor fisherman Jonas Persson:

> It all began last spring. Jonas had read in the papers about the Chinese. . . . It said in the paper that the Chinese are being brought up to hate. . . . They've nothing to eat, or anyway very little. They become soldiers and train for war. . . . In the article it said that . . . It's just a *question of time* until the Chinese have atom bombs. *They've nothing to lose.* That's what it said.[11]

In Tomas' inept effort to rescue Jonas from his deep depression, there is an intriguing reference to the very title of *Wild Strawberries*. In the acrid, derisive critique of Tomas and "Tomasism" by the oily organist Blom, there is an equally significant direct reference to the script of *Through a Glass Darkly*. For Tomas tells Jonas:

> We're alone, you and I. We've betrayed the only condition under which men can live: to live together. And that's why we're so poverty-stricken, joyless and full of fear. All this stink of an antique godliness! All this supernatural helplessness, this humiliating sense of sin! . . . You must live, Jonas. Summer's on the way. After all, the darkness won't last forever. You've got your strawberry beds, haven't you, and your flowering jasmine? What perfume! Long hot days. It's the earthly paradise, Jonas. It's something to live for! [12]

And Blom tells Märta:

> . . . his wife. A proper woodlouse. When she really got seriously ill, no one believed her. And then she died. That at least, I suppose, wasn't put on. And Tomas, he's got about as much knowledge of human nature as my old galoshes. He only had eyes for her. Lived for her, he did. Loved her like a lunatic. She, who hadn't a genuine feeling in her whole body, not an honest thought. That's what you can call love, if you like! Jesus! But it put an end to the vicar, it did. And now he's done for.
>
> *Blom leans even closer, he's almost in a good mood, lays a chubby hand on her shoulder.*
>
> BLOM: Listen, Märta. That's how it was with *that* love. (*Quotes*): "God is love, and love is God. Love is the proof of God's

existence. Love exists as something real in the world of
men and women." I know the jargon, as you can hear.
I've been an attentive listener to the vicar's outpour-
ings . . .[13]

Blom, of course, is quoting verbatim from the manifesto
proclaimed by the father David to his son Minus in *Through a
Glass Darkly*. It is an intriguing fact that Bergman has even
called upon the same actor, Gunnar Björnstrand, to play both
the role of David and the role of Pastor Tomas. Blom's quotation provides us surely with an incontestable evidence from
the scripts themselves of exactly what certainty, achieved in
Through a Glass Darkly, Bergman wanted to unmask in *Winter
Light*. It is precisely the humanistically restrictive pseudo-
identification of love with God. The characters involved in
Through a Glass Darkly had all fondly imagined, each in an
individual way, that they saw indeed, albeit "through a glass
darkly," a rescue for mankind. It was enough to know, even in
the rubble of the collapse of former geometric theological certitude, that there was a human sociological certainty, the conviction that the mere fact that "love exists as something real in the
world of men" is, if not a proof of the existence of God, at
least a safe temporary haven in which every questing, tormented
human seeker can let his "emptiness," his "dirty hopelessness,
rest." Now that certainty is unmasked for what it is: a romantic
nonsensical humanism, unable to purge man's despair or comfort his desperate loneliness and fear. The sociological concern
and involvement, the humanistically vapid cosmopolitanism
and Waldenism Tomas tries to evoke before Jonas—these are
not enough. If man is to be redeemed, it must be by the strong,
desperate, rending *Caritas* of the God who cloaks himself in a
dreadful silence in the face of all man's pertinent and imperti-
nent questionings, who in this film speaks only once, in the
majestic thunder of the waterfall that drowns out the solicitous
chatter of the human establishment around the corpse of a
suicide.

Tomas explicitly evokes "the earthly paradise" where the jasmine gives a fragrant smell and the strawberries are a testimony of fruitfulness and flavor. No more need here for that "stink of an antique godliness, all this supernatural helplessness, this humiliating sense of sin." But in fact the sequel is the suicide of Jonas; and the buoyant vision of Tomas fades instantly on the spot into a racking attack of feverish chills:

> TOMAS: I don't feel well, I've got a fever. Everything's swaying about. I . . . I can't collect my thoughts. I'm ill. The fact is, I'm in a wretched state.
>
> *He lays his arms on the table and supports his forehead on his hands. Shaken by feverish chills, he moans faintly, the sweat breaks out on his forehead and temples and on his hands. Gradually the attack subsides. He becomes quieter. When he looks up Jonas has vanished. No footsteps, no sound of a door closing. No wind in cracks and crevices. Complete silence. He drags himself over to the window.*
>
> *No car, no traces. Not a sound. The snow falls softly and steadily.*
>
> *God's silence, Christ's twisted face, the blood on the brow and hands, the soundless shriek behind the bared teeth.*
>
> *God's silence.*[14]

This grisly and dreadful picture is in savage contrast with the superficial, faded, almost bumptious simplism of the closing hymn sung at the communion service. That hymn had expressed the neat, geometric certainty of a time no easier in its everyday problematic than the present but not yet troubled by the loping shadow of the atheistic doubts that plague man now. That hymn had gaily simpered:

> Last, my God, I pray Thee,
> Take my hand in Thine
> Lead me, gently lead me,
> To the land divine,
> And when woes are ended,
> And my course is run
> Thou wilt take my spirit
> Home, O Lord, to Thine.[15]

But it is of cardinal significance that the features and presence of the incarnate God dominate both the sweetest and the bitterest moments of this film. The communion service is *his* banquet; and it is *he* who grimaces in deadly torment over Tomas' racking doubt and lapse into short-lived atheistic liberation.

Highly significant, further, is the fact that Bergman uses precisely the communion act itself to introduce the chief characters and the chorus of the film. Five times the chill-wracked pastor tenders the bread: "The Body of our Lord Jesus Christ, which was given for thee." And five times he tenders the cup: "Christ's blood, shed for thee." The rest of the ceremony is permeated by the explicitly invoked presence of Christ:

> He is the Lamb of our Passover, sacrificed for us, who beareth all the world's sins, even unto death. And even as He hath overcome death and risen again and liveth forever, so shall we and all who put their trust in Him, through Him overcome sin and death and inherit eternal life. . . . We thank Thee for Thy salvation, which Thou hast prepared for us through Jesus Christ. . . . prepare us rightly to celebrate the memory of our Savior . . . Let us now pray together, even as our Lord Jesus hath taught us. . . . Lamb of God, Son of the Father, that takest away the sins of the world. . . . The grace and peace of our Lord Jesus Christ be with you all. . . . Give us grace so to commemorate Jesus on earth, that we may be partakers in Thy great communion in heaven.[16]

These are all, of course, liturgical texts; but the significant fact is that in this film Bergman has not scrupled to devote the first ten minutes of running time to such a protracted presentation of the central Christian act. No mere series of rapid allusions or scene-evoking close-ups but a continuous portrayal. There is a strong sustained intent to evoke the liturgico-sacramental dimension and the figure of Christ.

To be sure, Bergman indicates with deft directions the failure, the utter poignant failure, of the liturgical act and operation meaningfully to communicate to most of the tiny congregation:

> *The congregation get up. Most stand dumbly with expression-less faces. . . . Finally, Tomas goes up to Märta Lundberg. Smiling ironically, she is waiting. . . . The congregation get up and the organ puffs and squeaks. Someone drops a walking stick on the floor.*[17]

But there is the poor hunchback sexton, Algot Frövik, who, after receiving the chalice, *"stands quite still with his eyes closed and a serious expression on his face, from which the pain has departed."* [18]

There is the pathetic Mrs. Persson, who *"takes the means of grace with quiet emotion."* [19]

Later in the day (and in the film) there is a drastic confrontation in Märta's schoolroom between the pastor and the little boy who has come to get his forgotten comic book. Better than a thousand-word descriptive exposition, this harsh, shy exchange brings into lurid focus the debilitating extent to which the faith has faltered and died in this little hamlet:

TOMAS: What's the dog's name?
BOY: Jim.
TOMAS: Is he yours?
BOY: No.
TOMAS: Then he's your older brother's? The one who's being confirmed this year!
BOY: Yes.
TOMAS: Are you going to come to confirmation class?
BOY: No.
TOMAS: Oh, why not?
BOY (*embarrassed*): Don't know.

> *The boy, who has picked a lurid comic out of his desk and is standing in front of Tomas, looking out of the window, twists and scrapes his snow-covered boot.*

TOMAS: Does your brother think the classes are boring?
BOY: Mm. I dunno.
TOMAS: What are you going to be when you grow up?

The boy shifts his glance and looks Tomas straight between the eyes with an expression of indulgent disdain.

BOY: Spaceman.[20]

Yet it would be grotesquely superficial to imagine this film as a lampoon of institutional religion or even a sad threnody for lost and dying faith. All such considerations are entirely peripheral to the film's main thrust. And that is the simultaneous probing of the religious dynamic and the dynamic of the relationship between Tomas and Märta. There is the strictest parallel. For Märta is identifiably the God-mouthpiece in this daring poetic probe into the significance and demands of the Incarnation.

In the context of such sustained insistence on the incarnational-eucharistic act of union, it would be risky in the extreme to dismiss as merely sociological or personal human commentary the charged dialogue between Tomas and Märta just after the Mass:

MÄRTA   (*smiling*): A Sunday at the very bottom of the vale of tears.
TOMAS: I don't feel too well.
MÄRTA: Want me to be sorry for you?
TOMAS: Yes, please.
MÄRTA   (*smiles*): Then you'll have to marry me.
TOMAS   (*sighs, closes his eyes*): Oh, I see.
MÄRTA: You could so easily marry me.
TOMAS: What for?
MÄRTA: Then I wouldn't have to go away from here.[21]

To mankind is being held out a redemption and deliverance from his equivocal state, his loneliness and helplessness, his lack of love. But the price is a union more intimate than any merely irregular association. She who has been exploited as mistress demands, as the price of her operational pity, the status of spouse.

Märta in fact has recourse to a lengthy letter to communicate her feelings and problems to Tomas. The reading of this missive entire by Tomas on screen with the camera focusing exclusively on Märta's face is surely one of the most unusual sequences ever shown in any film; and its unremitting exhaustiveness signals imperiously that this document is a key as vital as the eucharistic action of the morning to the message of the film. On the surface, indeed, the letter reads as a somewhat pathetic though not unattractive outpouring of a muddled woman's heart; and this dimension must certainly not be neglected on pain of distorting oversimplification or schematization. But with this reservation and in the light of the eucharistic banquet just concluded, a scarlet thread of soteriological meaning can be traced through the ramblings of this woman who says pointedly that she does not believe and never has believed in God. Her persistent eczema can, on one level, be identified as a sure symptom of emotional unbalance and neurosis. But on another level, this eczema and Tomas' reaction to it is strongly reminiscent of Isaias' prophetic vision:

> There is no beauty in him, nor comeliness; and we have seen him, and there was no sightliness, that we should be desirous of him. He was despiesd and rejected of men, a man of sorrows and acquainted with grief. And we hid as it were our faces from him. He was despised and we esteemed him not. Surely he hath borne our infirmities and carried our sorrows; and we have thought of him as it were a leper, and as one struck by God and afflicted (Is. 53:2–4).

For poor Märta writes:

> My skin had flaked off and my palms were like open sores. . . . The open sores affected you unpleasantly. You couldn't pray, the whole situation simply disgusted you. Now, after the event, I understand you; but you never understood me. After all, we'd been living together quite a while, almost two years. One would think this represented a certain little capital in our poverty, in tendernesses exchanged, and in our clumsy attempts to get round the lovelessness of our relationship. And then, when the eczema broke out on my forehead and around my scalp, it wasn't long before I noticed you were avoiding me.[22]

Halfway through her letter, Märta makes a strong explicit reference to Tomas' crucial religious weakness:

And when I came into contact with your faith, it seemed to me obscure and neurotic, in some way cruelly overcharged with emotion, primitive. One thing in particular I couldn't understand, your peculiar indifference to the gospels and to Jesus Christ.[23]

In effect, Tomas represents that most pathological and subversive of all phenomena: a deliberate pre-Christian in the age and dispensation of Jesus Christ. And here the parallel between the God-man relationship and the Tomas-Märta liaison is especially striking: the reason Tomas cannot respond to the living and suffering Märta at his side is because of his virtually necrophiliac attachment to his dead wife. The reason Tomas cannot respond to Christ is because he insists on clutching to him the selfish security of a pre-Christian notion of the Mighty Lord of Hosts who fends especially for Tomas Eriksson and never exposes him to the awful drama of the free love-assignment of a free rational creature! Indeed Tomas himself shows that the letter has made an impression on him, when he tells Jonas, just after reading it, of precisely this selfish utilitarianism in his relation with God, mentions his late wife's connivance with him in shoring up his dream, and then adds flatly: "My indifference to the gospel message, my jealous hatred of Jesus." [24]

And the end of Märta's long rambling letter pinpoints with daring poetic precision the very God-side of the incarnational phenomenon:

> I've realised I love you, I prayed for a task to apply my strength to, and got it, too. It's you. . . . I love you and I live for you. Take me and use me. Beneath all my false pride and independent airs I've only one wish: to be allowed to live for someone else. It will be terribly difficult.[25]

Märta is, to be sure, sniveling and not a little neurotic; but one would hardly expect the "sweet story of old" to be pictured in this context in unalloyed form! It would be atrocious cinema. The solid fact remains, however temerariously blasphemous it may sound, that Märta is precisely offering Tomas the full Eucharist and he is being a bad and guilty communicant, eating and drinking unworthily unto damnation. For she is offering him her body and entire saving personality; and he insists on stopping short of complete communion, stopping short at the formalistic and noncommittal comfort of the purely mechanical communion of fornication.

Now in the dynamic of the entire film there is no faintest doubt that Märta, athwart all her peccadilloes, is incomparably stronger than Tomas. Her dire prediction may indeed be tinged by a bit of hurt pride, but it is nonetheless crushingly accurate:

> What'll become of you—without me? . . . Oh no, you won't be able to manage. You'll go under, dearest Tomas. Nothing can save you. You'll hate the life out of yourself.[26]

It would be fatal to a proper understanding of this soteriological drama not to investigate very attentively Tomas' objections, in their superficial cogency and their basic bankruptcy:

> I'm tired of your loving care, your fussing over me, your good advice, your little candlesticks and table-runners. I'm fed up with your short-sightedness and your clumsy hands, your anxiousness and your timid ways when we make love. You force me to occupy myself with your physical condition, your bad stomach, your eczemas, your periods, your frostbitten cheek. Once and for all I must get out of all this rubbish, this junkheap of idiotic circumstances. I'm sick and tired of the whole thing, of everything to do with you.[27]

Tomas Eriksson can rant and posture all he will—he cannot evade the simple evidence that what he wants is not a person but a sort of symbol or mechanical comforter. He will not accept, least of all in the religious dimension, the awful dark night of the dialogue of love with *a Person*. And there is a deeper reason even than his overfastidious selfishness. He screams it at Märta when she inquires about his dead wife:

> I loved her! D'you hear that? I loved her! But I don't love you. Because I loved my wife. . . . I loved her and she was everything you can never be, and which you're always trying to be. The way you mimic her behaviour is just an ugly parody.[28]

To which Märta's calm and devastating reply is: "I didn't even know her."

Because man has persistently chosen to cling to a dream of his own utter autonomy and to worship the "woodlouse" of his own "earthly paradise," he is unable to grasp the saving "Body of our Lord Jesus Christ, which was given for thee."

Yet Tomas is equally unable entirely to cast off Märta, even as he is utterly incapable of persisting in his atheistic emancipation.

> TOMAS: Want to come to Frostnäs with me? *(Pause)* I'll try not to be nasty.
>
> *She looks up. Her face wears a shut-in, stern expression.*
>
> MARTA *(stiffly)*: Will you, really? Or is it just that some new fright's flown into you?
> TOMAS: Do as you like; but I'm asking you to come.
> MARTA: Of course. Naturally I'll come. I haven't any choice, have I? [29]

For Tomas has a basic trenchant honesty beneath all his posturings and pettiness. What Isak Borg nostalgically quested after and Vogler ruthlessly probed for, what David thought he had glimpsed "through a glass darkly," that Tomas Eriksson squarely faces as unattainable because insubstantial: the hope of man-engendered human salvation from loneliness, lovelessness, and fear. Tomas faces this cardinal fact of the human equation with "a pale and anxiety-filled face" as he intones his desperate doxology to total transcendence.

In the journey of the human SPIRIT from ANXIETY to JOY (the three words that will figure at a crucial point in *The Silence*), there can be no reliance placed in a superficially passive demanding surrender to a paternalistic deity who manipulates this creature merely for his own aggrandizement nor yet in a restrictively humanistic activism that would seek to redeem man by his own unaided efforts. Rather there must be the acceptance of the challenge of free created love, which, in the dispensation of the Fall and the incarnational redemption, is the challenge to follow Christ to Calvary singing a hymn of praise and trust to God, the transfiguring Master who yet wills that his human creatures shall collaborate in their own redemption.

The silence of God hangs heavy over *Winter Light*, but its focal point shifts, in Algot's exposition, to the awful rendezvous point foreshadowed in *The Magician* and here openly revealed: Calvary, where hangs "Christ's twisted face, the blood on the brow and hands, the soundless shriek behind the bared teeth." For the lesson of Calvary is not unidimensional. To the truth that free rebellious man must ultimately crucify his God, there answers, as deep to deep, the God-truth that a free God, a freedom-loving God, can show his free human creature how to find salvation only by himself going the whole way with that creature. Algot's evocation of Christ's agony is a startling revelation of an insight more traditional theists would grasp if only they would leave off their cramped pusillanimous Monophysitic geometricization in their mistaken apologetic for God: the free incarnate God must show man the road to salvation by himself tasting of man's worst and most horrifying doubt, atheism.

What is lost sight of is precisely that God is Person, supremely Person, explosively trinitarianly Person, *Persona* indeed. And because Person, therefore powerful to do and to suffer as person and so to redeem and enlighten his personal creatures. And in this dynamic, in the lurid light of Calvary, a staggering truth is revealed to those who can see (though, perhaps, in order to see, they must, like old Algot, themselves have suffered a great deal). This truth is that the multidimensional silence of God can close not only over man but over the incarnate God himself; and that in the light of his dereliction man is no longer alone, for his most intimate fear has been taken up and transformed and transfigured by openhearted love into boundless trust.

Here is the ultimate answer to the silence of God, the only answer that is redemptive and adequate to God's challenge. For that silence, in the mystery of freedom, impenetrable to mortal eyes, is itself a supreme act of willing trust in freedom, in free creatures; and those creatures must rise to justify the magnanimity of their Creator. As they abandoned him in pride, so they must find him in humility with their freedom intact and their spurs won by pain.

It was the Lamb "standing as it were slain" (Rev. 5:6) who in John's apocalyptic vision was found "worthy . . . to take the book and open the seals thereof: because thou wast slain and hast redeemed us to God, in thy blood, out of every tribe, and tongue, and people, and nation. And hast made us to our God a kingdom and priests, and we shall reign on the earth" (Rev. 5:9–10). And John tells us further that "when he had opened the seventh seal, there was silence in heaven as it were for half an hour" (Rev. 8:1).

For this is the drama that must still be played out to its highly uncertain conclusion. The witness is there in this Bergman cycle, from that moment in *Winter Light* when we see the tormented priest underneath that abiding presence of "Christ's twisted face, the blood on the brow and hands, the soundless shriek behind the bared teeth." The challenge is clear: it is not the simple challenge of mere passive acceptance of this suffering Savior; not even the mere demand for penance and reparation. Man, epitomized by Tomas, *must become as that Christ.* Shouldering the burden of created freedom and responding to the call of the transforming God, man must mount the cross and himself proclaim that God is holy in all his ways.

The last line of *Winter Light* must surely strike the viewer with a staggering sense of dramatic power. It is like those greatest lines of Greek tragic verse that strike the very nerves of man with pity and terror. For one thing, it comes so unexpectedly; for another, it is liturgical, as was the film's opening; and finally, it is somehow felt to grow out of the whole inner dynamic of the film. Tomas, who cannot yet say yes to Märta, whom he has seen, seems for a trembling instant able and ready to say yes to God, whom he has not seen.

For the proclamation of the glory of God widens man's own horizon immeasurably, cures him definitively of the pernicious tendency to demand exhaustively satisfying rational explanations which cannot be given because man is not a closed mechanical circle but a perpetual opening onto transcendence. The proclamation of God's glory in the midst of human doubt and pain effects a rectification of perspective: man himself realizes suddenly that his own destiny is neither mere restoration of lost innocence nor Promethean rebellion against allegedly trameling fetters but rather the perpetual assignment of transcending. Man's present state is there not to be merely mechanically rectified but to be overcome.

The innermost nexus and nucleus of the cryptic message is inimitably expressed in Märta's simple words to Tomas. It is bound intimately to a recurrent theme of these films, an inseparable accompaniment of the faith problematic, of the certitude problematic, and therefore of the silence-of-God problematic. What Märta tells Tomas, God is persistently telling man out of his great silence: "You must learn to love." [30]

SUFFERING

The Silence

The powers are too strong for us, I mean the *monstrous* powers.

A strangely assorted trio is compelled by the sickness of one member to stop at a strange city in a strange land with a strange language. There is Ester, the elder sister, a translator by profession, who is visited by horrible fits of coughing indicative of a mortal ailment; Anna, her rebellious, sultry younger sister; and little Johan, Anna's ten-year-old son, a bright and inquisitive boy, lacerated by the sullen strife prevailing between his mother and his aunt.

Arrived in the hotel, Ester is put to bed and Anna allows Johan to scrub her back in the bath before packing him off to bed for an afternoon nap. Ester cannot sleep; she summons an old waiter to order a fresh supply of brandy, has great difficulty communicating, learns the word KASI=hand in the strange tongue of the city, uses her own hand to masturbate herself, and falls into a fitful sleep.

Johan has wakened, well before his mother, from the afternoon nap. He ventures forth into the hotel corridor and into a series of strange polyvalent adventures with the old waiter, a troupe of dwarfs, and again with the old waiter, who opens a big black wallet and shows him photos: a house behind a big tree, an old woman in a coffin, children of various ages.

Anna wakes up and tells Ester ungraciously that she is going out for air. Ester suffers an especially acute attack of choking, falls to the floor, is picked up by the old waiter and put to bed. Anna meanwhile has picked up a husky young waiter whom she brings back to the hotel to her room, mainly to spite Ester. Johan has returned and been detailed to keep Ester company. Aunt and nephew cannot communicate immediately for the very simple reason that Ester is asleep and snoring. Johan investigates some cards on her desk on which are written three more words in the strange language; he has a terrifying view of a tank lumbering down the city street. Ester wakes and Johan offers to put on a Punch and Judy show for her. Punch talks in a funny language because he is frightened. Johan throws himself into his aunt's arms, sobbing bitterly; she tries to shield and comfort him. Anna meanwhile is caressing hips, stomach and genitals of her wordless bed companion, the young waiter. She expresses the wish, which the young man does not understand, that Ester were dead.

Later, about to go to bed for the night, Johan chats with his aunt a little about why she is a translator: she promises to write him down the words she has learned of the language of this strange city. Anna and Ester have a grueling spat: Anna accuses Ester of trying to manage her; Ester retorts that Anna cannot manage on her own. Anna accuses Ester of an exaggerated sense of her own importance; Ester counters with a bitter denunciation of Anna's morals, merging into a desperate and trembling plea that Anna stop fornicating with every comer; Anna taunts Ester with jealousy of Anna's lovers. Finally Ester goes to her room: Anna bursts into wild laughter, followed by heavy weeping; Ester suffers a desperate attack and a thin stream of blood runs quietly down over her chin, flecks her skirt, and drips onto the carpet.

Morning finds Anna disinterested in her night partner with his black growth of beard. She tries to open the door and discovers that Ester has collapsed against it: Anna reaches out her arms toward her stricken sister's head.

At noon Ester is ministered to by the old waiter as Anna and Johan go out for a bite to eat. Ester painfully scrawls out a message for Johan, containing the promised words in the strange tongue of the city. She listens to a child crying in the street below, babbles to the old waiter (who understands nothing but is pathetically eager to help this poor sick woman). Ester tells him about her aesthetic (mainly olfactory) objection to semen, bitterly laments the part she has to play, remarks on the strength of the *"monstrous* powers," and recalls her father's strange words just before his death ("Now it's eternity, Ester"). She is seized with a horrible fit of choking suffocation, sobs bitterly that she does not want to die alone, screams that the doctor should have come long ago, gasps out a call for help to her mother as her consciousness ebbs.

Johan is frightened as he creeps in to find his aunt in such a state, but she reassures him and gives him the secret message. Anna has decided to travel on home with little Johan; Ester will follow later. The parting is almsot banal. Ester's face is a death's head; she is alone in the strange city in the strange room with the old waiter who understands only that he is in the presence of a suffering and abandoned woman.

The last scene shows us Anna and Johan in the train, traveling onward in the direction of home, Johan is painstakingly trying to decipher his aunt's secret message.

The silence in this film seems scarcely any longer the mere silence of God: it is surely the utter cessation of all communication, even between mortals. Steel-shrouded tanks lumber

119

down a city street; sisters speak to each other only to lacerate; aunt and nephew grope unsuccessfully for communication and tenderness; mother and son are worlds apart; the boy is abandoned repeatedly or simply left to vanish somewhere while mother is about her business of fornication; a lust partner cannot communicate in any language other than the neuromuscular one, and Anna finds this especially delightful ("How nice it is we don't understand each other").

Man has no meaningful contact with God, said *The Seventh Seal*; man is loveless, said *Wild Strawberries*; out of his love-lessness man makes contact with dark powers, said *The Magician*; the darkest of these powers surge up from man's own inmost heart and issue in sterile narcissistic tragedy, said *Through a Glass Darkly*; man must break out of this dark circle and can do so only by some drastic affirmation of God, said *Winter Light*; this affirmation, however, must be free and involve total commitment without any immediate responsive powering, says *The Silence*.

The very real affection of Anna for Ester is most clearly underlined in the script and all too often neglected by the hasty evaluations that see only the surface and conclude to such ludicrously inadequate explanations as sibling rivalry and lesbian overtones of aggression. Anna explicitly asserts her real affection for Ester in the course of the only protracted conversation in this entire film so sown with the constellations of silence: "I always thought you were right. And tried to be like you. And I admired you." [1]

But Anna's affection for Ester is at constant war with her own frantic and distracted search for personal independent identity. Unquestionably Bergman feels deep sympathy for the tormented younger sister, Anna. She is to be despised and reprehended not for her desperate search for identity but rather for her complete imperviousness to the fact that she can never attain to that identity in battle with her elder sister, any more than man can in battle with God. As Ester sadly remarks after one of Anna's furious outbursts of rejection and insult: "How do you want us to live, then? After all, we own everything in common."[2]

The first film of the trilogy examines a sociological situation which is complex enough in all conscience, against a deliberately muted background of the spider behind the wallpaper. The intelligent humanists in this film do not even want to admit that this behind-the-wallpaper dimension exists. And so at the end, by the awful grace of God, they find their sociological certainty. It is encapsulated in the formula: Let us love one another! It rejects in outrage the spider God.

The second film of the trilogy unmasks this sociological certainty. Such entirely and restrictively human or humanized affection is powerless to solve geopolitical problems (the Chinese with hate in their hearts and the bomb in their hands). This all-too-human affection is even destructive, as Blom warns Märta when he inveighs against the necrophiliac and impotent Tomas:

> For your own sake, Märta. You who can move, get out as quick as you can. Everything here at Mittsunda and Frostnäs is in the grip of death and decay.[3]

Mankind must learn from the thunder of the cataract roaring around the corpse of a voluntary suicide the awful wisdom of Christ's austere words: "A new commandment I give unto you: that you love one another, *as I have loved you*." And how was that? Giving all yet forcing nothing, demanding all yet seizing nothing. We are up against the ultimate created mystery, the darkest and most luminous at once, *created freedom*. And it is the reason for the silence of God.

The third film draws forth the spider behind the wallpaper into a presence at once more luminous and more terrifying than even that hidden spider known only to the mystic or even that thunderous waterfall heard distractedly by the would-be atheist.

As the palpable silence of God takes shape before us, it is the brooding elder sister with the enormous eyes.

Ester, as we have already indicated, is instructed by the stage directions to write three words in the strange foreign language of the city of their stopover, the language which, as professional translator, she is impelled to interpret for and teach to her young nephew:

> *Johan goes over to the window, which is ajar, and looks down into the street, all empty now and silent. . . .*
> *Scared by the dull, anxious stillness, he withdraws his head.*
> *On the writing desk lie a few pieces of paper, scribbled all over in Ester's microscopic handwriting.*
> *One or two, however, are written in large printed capitals. There is HADJEK = spirit, MAGROV = anxiety, fear, KRASGT = joy.*[4]

Not even this detail is fortuitous in a Bergman film. The dynamic thrust of the trilogy is the odyssey of the created human spirit from deadly fear to quiet joy. But God's joy is not our contented-cow happiness of psychic health and decent accommodation to a pleasant suburban society, just as the incarnate God must say: "Peace I leave with you; my peace I give unto you. *Not as the world giveth, give I unto you.*" The joy that rests in God is the diligent joy that tries painfully and cautiously to decipher his secret message, that knows it is this God who has the message, that the message does not originate and bubble forth from the depths of man's own psyche but comes from outside to him, from outside his entire dimension.

Ester has been stricken in the train by a violent bout of her chronic illness. This forces the trio to make their stopover in the strange city in the strange land. Anna's activities, aside from lacerating verbal jousts with Ester, can be very simply and briefly described: she goes on a lust hunt into the city and picks up a young waiter with whom she can converse only neuromuscularly; she says to him: "How nice you are. How nice it is we don't understand each other."[5]

Anna taunts Ester constantly with this lust affair and displays a biting cynicism and sarcasm about Ester's illness: "When she's ill. She's always ill. When she's ill, she wants to decide every-thing. Then I'm a half-wit."[6]

And finally, after Ester has suffered a particularly devastating attack, Anna coldly and sullenly leaves her in the lonely hotel room and takes the train home with Johan.

In the tormented tensional relationship between these two so completely disparate sisters is bodied forth the dynamic of the God-man relationship as that dynamic approaches its definitive climax. Anna has clearly invoked the paradigm of voluntary atheism in her spitefully intense outburst during the macabre lust scene. The stage directions are calculated to ensure that this ominous little phrase shall be as cruel and sordidly blas-phemous as possible.

> *Her hand caresses his hip, his stomach, feels between his legs.*
>
> ANNA: I wish Ester was dead.[7]

Again here, as in *Winter Light,* but in far more nauseatingly dirty fashion, man is clinging to an idol, any idol, a muscular bull-idol picked up in a sidewalk café, in order to shield himself against the love of God.

In Ester's brief, poignant conversation with Anna, it is crystal clear that a serene nondestructive possessive tenderness is warning against God's most mysterious opponent, the ulti-mately free human will:

> ANNA: If only I could understand why I've been so scared.
> ESTER: Scared?
> ANNA: Scared of you.
>
> *She sinks her head deeply, affirmatively, then straightens her back, gathers her housecoat about her.*
> *Seeing Ester's look she gives an enigmatic smile, leaves the room, silently and softly closes the door. At once Ester stops work, stares out of the window at the sun-burned wall of the house opposite. A mortal fear of death sweeps over her, from be-tween her clenched white teeth escapes a faint moan.*[8]

God is concerned that the death of God may indeed become a reality if man persists in his free rejection of all advances.

123

In another brief interchange, Ester queries sadly from her side: "Why've we got to torment each other?" and Anna fiercely counters, with all the false assurance of rebellious man, who has seen he can hurt God: "You aren't tormenting me." [9]

In the most revealing interchange, already alluded to in part, the whole spectrum of the God-man relationship is explored in a few staccato outbursts.

Anna lashes out at the transcendence and self-sufficiency of God in words evocative of man's drastic revolt against his creaturely status:

> When Father was alive he decided things. And we obeyed him. Because we had to. When Father died you thought you could carry on in the same way. And went on about your principles, how meaningful everything was, how important! But it was just a lot of poppycock. (*Pause*) D'you know why? I'll tell you why. It was all in aid of your self-importance. You can't live without your sense of your own importance. And that's the truth of it. You can't bear it if everything isn't "a matter of life and death" and "significant" and "meaningful" and I don't know what else.

God's answer emerges calmly out of Ester's quiet rejoinder: "How do you want us to live, then? After all we own everything in common."

Now man strikes out viciously at this overpowering Creator, dredging up out of the murky cauldron of his own half-understood subconscious intuitions two entirely perverted formulations of transcendent truth: "I always thought you were right. And tried to be like you. And I admired you." And now comes the first perversion: "I didn't realise you disliked me." It is immediately followed by the second perversion: "Yes! And in some way I can't understand, you're scared of me."

God can only reply: "I'm not scared, Anna. I love you."

And as this scene ends with man's furious dismissal of God ("Go away! Get out! Leave me alone!"), it is God who replies: "Poor Anna."

The scenario here is highly revealing and has been faithfully translated onto the screen:

> *Ester gets up, goes to the door. Her face is completely calm. Its petrified expression of pain has dissolved and been succeeded by an almost imperceptible smile.*
>
> *She looks at her sister, without superiority, sympathetically, with tenderness.*
>
> *Slowly she closes the door behind her.*[10]

In fact this epitome of rebellious man can only approach God with even a minimum of meaningfulness and relevance when asking for a concrete and specific favor:

ANNA *(in a low voice)*: Johan was going to ask you for some cigarettes. Mine are finished.
ESTER: On the desk.
ANNA: Can I take a few?
ESTER: Of course.
ANNA: Thanks. Nice of you.[11]

But when it comes to any really vital matters, especially matters involving a volitional decision, man rears up snappishly on his hind legs:

ANNA: D'you think you matter in the least? I mean, what you do or say?

Ester contemplates her legs, shrugs her shoulders.

ANNA: Whoever put that notion into your head? That it's up to you to decide?
ESTER *(coldly)*: You can't manage on your own.
ANNA: You think you can make my decisions for me, just like Father did. But you can't.
ESTER *(silent)*.
ANNA: You think I'm stupid, eh?
ESTER *(smiles)*: I don't think you're stupid.[12]

Yet Ester's evaluation is borne out by Anna's own pathetic inability to navigate as an adult human being. She tells shabby little exaggerated lies about her sex life simply to shock her sister. And all the while she moves through this smelly dunghill with uncertain and ungainly gait, profoundly inept and dissatisfied, pitiably self-destructive. Little Johan spots her fecklessness and forlornness, her rootless drifting, and articulates in his graphic child's way just what it is:

Johan sits down on the floor and draws his knees up under his chin, observing his mother, particularly her naked feet with their red lacquered toenails and strong high insteps. They move as it were of their own accord, steering themselves to and fro across the great worn carpet.

Anna catches sight of him in the cupboard mirror.

ANNA: What are you looking at?
JOHAN: I'm looking at your feet.
ANNA: Oh? Why?
JOHAN: They're walking around with you, all by themselves.[13]

It is not merely man who is destitute and forlorn. The sick and bleeding specimen Ester is a highly, almost blasphemously anthropomorphized God. But there is a profound reason for this, a profound ontological point at issue: for this God has not merely been willing to take to himself our human nature; he has also been willing, in his "translation drive," to expose himself to our abuse. It is not simply that God can and does progressively reveal the beauty of his divine love and its agony, in himself incarnate, to man the seeker; there is the human contribution likewise to be borne in mind: man, the free potential rebel, can and does really lacerate this God, even though the ultimate victim will always be man himself, not only, indeed not at all, the sorely flayed deity. It seems to me a matter of highest importance that Bergman allows—nay, even forces on the viewer—such a monstrous equivocation at film's end concerning Ester's state and fate. She has just told little Johan: "Don't be scared. I'm not going to die."[14] Now this might be taken as simply a laudable desire to reassure the youngster, were it not that it is followed immediately by Ester's crucial outburst:

I've written you a letter, as I promised. It's lying on the floor, if you can find it. *(Pause)* Johan! It's *important,* d'you understand! You must read it carefully. *(Pause)* It's all . . . It's all I . . . You'll understand.[15]

And when the entirely healthy, if quite frightened, boy stands that last moment after finding the letter at his apparently dying aunt's bedside, it is the desperately sick woman who comforts the exuberant boy: "Don't be frightened. You must be brave. (*Pause*) You must be brave."[16]

Surely there is a strong implication that the death of Ester has to do with utter inability to communicate rather than with physical dissolution. With her blood sister she has had no success whatever, only insulting, frustrating, and humiliating failure. Now in this letter to a child, Ester has shot her bolt. All communication depends on Johan's understanding Ester's note.

Johan is unquestionably the solitary figure of hope in this suffocating film. Free alike of his mother's bumptious assertiveness and of his aunt's shy melancholy, this little boy is yet lonely because his mother has no time to give him the affection he craves and his aunt makes him nervous, despite his obvious liking for her. Above all, Johan is terribly lacerated by the strife, the perpetual nagging and periodic explosions, between his aunt and his mother.

Johan is skittish with his aunt when she tries to caress him, but he manfully attempts to comfort her:

> *The conversation dies away. They fall silent. Ester puts out her hand and touches Johan's cheek and ear, mostly as a caress. He shies away with an expression of surprise but since his mouth is full of food doesn't say anything.*
>
> ESTER: You can go back to your own room if you've had enough.
> JOHAN: Thanks for the food. I'm dreadfully full up.
>
> *He keeps a polite distance; jumps down off the bed, goes toward the other room.*
>
> ESTER: Leave the door open, there's a good boy.
> JOHAN: I'll make you a lovely painting if you like.
>
> *Ester nods. Tenderness for the boy, and fear. All these confused thoughts.*

127

JOHAN: You mustn't worry. Mum'll soon be back. Besides, I'm here.[17]

But after this amazing child has foraged inquisitively through hotel corridors, met and struck up an ingenuous friendship with a troupe of laughing dwarfs, been drawn into a fleeting intimacy by a sad-faced old waiter, he encounters in a savage horrifying little scene the palpable presence of man's evil and dereliction; he runs to his aunt and, after a last brave attempt to play the man, throws himself into her arms sobbing out the terror of his child's heart.

This palpable symbol of human horror is none of the conventional symbols of deviation or disintegration (neither dwarfs nor doddering old waiter) but the objectification of human destructiveness and human secretiveness, a tank:

> Johan puts out the desk lamp and stands listening in the dark. Through the soles of his feet he can feel the floor quivering slightly. He hears a faint tinkling, notices that a drinking glass is rattling against its carafe. Through the silence a rattling rumbling murmur rises and falls, as of a heavy machine at work. He clambers up into the window and looks each way down the street. At first it is as empty and deserted as before.
>
> But after a few moments a shapeless shadow frees itself out of the dusk by the church steps. Takes shapes, swings with a heavy crashing noise down the narrow street and rolls slowly down towards the next side-street.
>
> It stops, all sounds cease, the glass no longer trembles against the side of its carafe, the floor no longer quivers beneath Johan's feet. The tank stands motionless. Expectant. Threatening. No sign of anyone.
>
> Johan turns his glance to Ester, sees she's awake and is observing him with a strange wide-eyed gaze.[18]

Initially Johan attempts to carry off the situation with his presentation of his Punch and Judy show. But this very drama suddenly becomes too much for the boy.

The puppets fight. The old woman screams and weeps. Punch rages. In the end the little old woman dies, or at least disappears behind the end of the bed.

JOHAN: Now he doesn't know what to do, because the old woman is dead.
PUNCH *(livid)*: Ulipiss pissipisspiss!
ESTER: What's he saying?
JOHAN: How should I know? He's talking in a funny language. Because he's frightened.[19]

In the boy's mind, at the level of human experience, there undoubtedly swirls a bewildering mélange of impressions: the constant quarrels between his mother and aunt; the kaleidoscope of his strange and somewhat disconcerting adventures during his reconnaissance of the old hotel (the pathetic dwarfs with their stunted efforts at friendliness; the picture of a body in a coffin which the old waiter has shown him; the self-important little man with the "sharp dark voice" who reprimanded the dwarfs; the dizzy expanses of the hotel corridor with its "mouldy chill"; and overriding all other impressions, the threatening attitude in the city square, the ominous opaque presence of the lumbering tank); his own ambivalent reaction in the face of his little adventures ("a shiver of anxiety, an elated desire for adventure"[20]); and his imperious need for protection against the horror of the tank and for some surrogate affection to fill the void of his mother's absentminded indifference. But at the level of God-talk there here emerges the dilemma of innocent man caught in the toils of guilty man's murder of God and torn between sympathy for his fellow and horror at the deicide perpetrated. The upshot is that the human child takes speedy refuge:

Punch leaps up and down.
Vanishes behind the end of the bed.
Silence.
Instead Johan, red in the face, rushes out, crying. He creeps up

to Ester in the bed, she throws her arms round him, over his head and cheeks, feels his breath, his thumping heart.

So they lie still together, listening to the rattling roar of the tank's motor. It swings round the corner, is gone.[21]

With Johan, Ester can give at least momentary and sporadic comfort and encouragement because the boy is open to her entirely, with no more reticence than the entirely normal shyness of the human boy; with Anna, however, Ester can make no headway whatsoever, for Anna is in full, sullen, and definitive revolt, relieved only by the odd, sluggish stirring of sisterly concern or merely human sympathy with a suffering woman. And at the very end of the film it is the same: indeed the dichotomy of human reaction to God's apparent silence is here heightened to a climactic pitch. The entire last scene is a fitting final prelude to the last fateful direct confrontation to occur in *Persona*. For in this last scene of *The Silence* there is a sense of impending doom, a drastic articulation of the two extremes of reaction possible to man challenged by God's apparent silence and necessarily cryptic revelation. Everything is on the knife's edge, as an ingenuous child puzzles over a secret message:

> *Darkness is falling over the town.*
>
> *A poisonous blue-black mass of cloud covers the sky and as the express, shortly after two o'clock, pulls out of the railway yards, the first heavy rain begins to fall.*
>
> *Anna and Johan are alone in a compartment. Each has a corner seat; neither speaks to the other. She has a book on her knee, but is not reading it. He has taken out Ester's letter and is studying it.*

> ANNA: What's that?
> JOHAN: Ester wrote me a letter.
> ANNA (*suspicious*): A letter. Let's see.

> *Reluctantly, Johan gives her the crinkled paper with the incomprehensible foreign words.*
>
> *Anna shrugs, hands it back to her son. He takes it from her and reads it, whispering.*

> It gets darker and darker, the rain squirts down over the windowpanes. Anna opens the window and lets the water splash over her hands and face. Johan's face is pale with the effort of trying to understand the strange language. The secret message.[22]

I submit that this secret message can be articulated, with retrospective glance at *Through a Glass Darkly* and *Winter Light,* in these eminently theological terms: I have a love to offer you, a healing, serene, creative, and re-creative love. It is neither the fierce destructive love of helpless adolescence nor the self-interested love of romantic adulthood. Yet this love must destroy something in you, your skittish radical independence—you must not shy away from me so when I try to touch you! And this love does of course have its ultimate fulcrum in myself, for I am the only one who can translate into your language the strange and vital words of the book in the incomprehensible tongue.

The silence of God creates a negative impression in this film because the entire action is a savage explication of God's ultimate respect for human freedom. He will not, in a very real sense he cannot, force that freedom; yet not for one moment does he abate his claim! And as the film progresses, it becomes painfully clear that what Ester expects and demands and needs, for her creative and redemptive action on Anna and Johan alike, is not comforting and spontaneous affection, but the total submission to a free agent by a free agent, the willingness to admit radical inferiority and accept the sort of gift that can come only from one side of the partnership. Anna refuses utterly to make any such admission. But at film's end little Johan is studying, with open heart and knitted brow, the secret message. Johan, the child is still trying. So there is still hope. But meanwhile the silence of God must continue to endure.

In *The Silence* we are being shown the most secret face of God, his excruciating difficulties in communicating with that creature, man, who of all creatures, at least on our planet, is nearest or at least obscurely dearest to God, dearest even as rebel and groveler, dearest perhaps precisely because of this imperiled state. And *The Silence,* while climactic to the nucleus trilogy, which has viewed the God-man relationship and its dynamically crystallizing problematic from man's point of view, is transitional to *Persona,* which will view the same problematic from God's point of view.

In *The Silence* we witness God's weakest hour, as he battles the one virtually impregnable barrier that can block him, the drastic centrifugal thrust of the free human will in rebellion. In *Persona,* God, as portrayed by the utterly silent actress who is allegedly mentally ill, will return in all his beauty, serenity, and power; by then, however, he will have definitively given a hostage to fortune, in the person of a young son who persistently tries to make his parent's face come alive on a glass wall for all who lie in darkness and the shadow of death.

The prolonged death throes of Ester with their enigmatically equivocal outcome constitute a neural reproach to those theologians who insist too shrilly on God's utter impassibility. God is no longer impassible after the Incarnation, or else Jesus Christ is quite simply not God! The only way we can put it in our human jargon is to say that something has been taken up most intimately into God, a moist, shivering creature that can scream and gasp for air. Only in the light of Ester's gasping agony can the human viewer of the succeeding and most demanding film accept and even marvel at the beautiful serenity of Elizabeth Vogler.

Ester reveals, in one brief anguished outburst, the true origin of the death-wish that man first hurls out against God and then turns inward upon himself: "We try them out, one attitude after another, and find them all meaningless. The powers are too strong for us, I mean the *monstrous* powers." [23]

The shafts of illumination are converging. And a growing twinge of doubt and horrified surprise is gripping the viscera of the viewer. For the silence of God is subtly changing shape: it is no longer the deadness of the external firmament but rather the deafness of the inner ear. But what the ear cannot or will not hear, the eye cannot choose but see: "the soundless shriek behind the bared teeth."

The seeker who has followed the dynamic of the six films we have been treating must now be intuitively certain that the final step must be a head-on confrontation between a God explosively closer than man had ever imagined and the seeker who can no longer play the pleasant noncommital game of hide-and-seek. The silence of the cosmos, man's cosmos, is clamorous with the voice of God; if that voice is to be stilled into definitive silence, it must be by the free act of man.

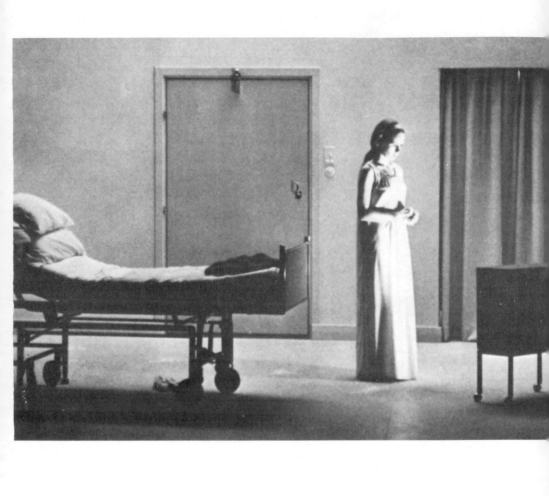

SEEING

Persona

Nothing, nothing, nothing at all!

Elizabeth Vogler is a surpassingly beautiful actress who has played many roles on many stages to the wild acclaim of a host of admirers. She suddenly falls silent during a rehearsal of her latest play and is perforce transported to a sanatorium for psychiatric treatment. To her case is assigned a pretty and lively young nurse, Alma, who is obviously considered by the hospital authorities to be the perfect medicine for this difficult and disturbing patient. Alma herself has a moment of queasiness at the outset but is reassured by her superior, the lady doctor in charge of the case of Elizabeth Vogler.

Alma has just given Elizabeth her injection when a woman's voice from the room radio begins moaning for forgiveness from an apparently outraged husband, in some soap opera. Elizabeth laughs until tears come to her eyes. The radio voice persists, calling on God in exactly the same terms as the knight did in *The Seventh Seal*. Elizabeth finds this hugely amusing, then

135

becomes thoughtful. Alma's efforts at drawing her out into a conversation on the demands of art on an artist are entirely unsuccessful. Alma tiptoes out. The room is in darkness.

Elizabeth watches television alone. She sees a fragment of a newsreel, a Buddhist in flames of fire suicide. Her eyes fill with tears.

Alma brings Elizabeth a letter. Elizabeth's obviously ineffectual and shadowy husband has written a somewhat whining missive, bewailing the collapse of their once happy marriage. He encloses a photograph of their young son. Elizabeth has listened unmoved to the letter; she now takes the photograph and studies it attentively. Then she tears it in two and gives Alma the pieces.

The lady doctor in charge decides Elizabeth and Alma should travel out to the doctor's own summer cottage near the sea: nature is a good healer, and there will be plenty of nature out there! Having arrived, Alma makes many overtures to Elizabeth in an effort to draw the enigmatically silent actress into conversation. Finally one evening, Alma decides to tell Elizabeth all about her own sexual peccadilloes, an unappetizing and banal experience at the beach with another girl and two boys who chance upon them and have mind-staggeringly meaningless intercourse with them there. Elizabeth listens patiently and not without sympathy but says not a word. But little Alma has babbled on so much that she is very tired. Her head is heavy. She seems to hear a clear low voice telling her she had better go to bed or else she will fall asleep at the table. She repeats the message aloud, somewhat bemused, and patters off to bed.

That night Alma sees Elizabeth come to visit her in her bedroom, get into bed with her, and conduct a highly significant conversation of few but supremely meaningful gestures to which Alma responds with equally few but decisive words. Next morning she inquires of Elizabeth if this visit really took place. Only silence and a slight negating shake of the head greets the question.

Alma is given a letter from Elizabeth to the doctor to post during a shopping trip; she opens and reads the letter and is distressed and enraged to find that Elizabeth finds her amusing, superficial, and banal, but tolerable and well-intentioned.

Now Alma becomes obsessed by the desire to hurt Elizabeth and by the equally strong desire to force her to speak. She places splintered glass where Elizabeth will step on it, throws boiling water at her face. Alternatively she begs Elizabeth almost tearfully to say something, anything. No success.

Elizabeth's shadowy husband comes to visit her and becomes involved in an amorous interchange with Alma, whom he mistakes temporarily for his wife. Elizabeth stares equably but pityingly at the strange scene.

Now begins a surrealistic quasi-hallucinatory exchange as Alma offers a diagnosis of Elizabeth's real problem, accusing her of utter lack of love and identification with her husband and above all with her child. The boundaries of personality between the two women threaten to dissolve. Even Alma is not sure who is who, whether she is speaking to Elizabeth with Alma's voice or to herself with Elizabeth's. Alma screams out in self-defense that she is not Elizabeth, never, never, never. A strange transposition of locale, almost out of time, shows nurse and patient in the same hospital room as at the outset. There is played out the climactic scene between God and man: Alma forces Elizabeth to repeat after her that there is nothing, nothing, nothing at all; patiently the tired low voice repeats the words. Elizabeth disappears from the scene and we are back in the summer cottage, where Alma is quickly packing her belongings; she runs happily down to the road to hail the bus back to the suburban life she has missed so much.

Even as the film had begun with a lightning series of Bergman symbols (nail-pierced hand, spider, winter woods), so it ends with a flickering of the filmstrip and the voice of the director in the background.

But just before that there is a curious scene, again out of

time, the other side of a bracket opened at the very outset of the movie: a young boy sits up on a slablike table and begins to trace the same features he traced at film's beginning: under his dextrous fingers the countenance of Elizabeth Vogler gradually comes into focus, in serene beauty upon a glass wall surrounding the boy and other sleepers.

I am deeply indebted to Mr. Bergman for his kindness in providing me with the Swedish manuscript of *Persona*, from which I have made my own English translation of the relevant excerpts of this film. It should be noted that no other script I have seen differs so radically from the finished film as does this *Persona* script. In the Preface, Bergman himself remarks:

> What I have here written seems to me most like a musical score which I believe I can orchestrate in the course of the filming, with the help of my associates.[1]

The single most arresting alteration is the drastic suppression in the film itself of the *reality* of Elizabeth's utterances. Whereas the script uses the technique of a continuing narration by the lady doctor to report undeniably real utterances of the "silent" actress, the film relegates such utterances to the half world of dream and fantasy, with Elizabeth appearing to speak from a tape recorder or perhaps only in imagination (for, on more than one occasion, she is shown with unmoving lips as the brief sentences are uttered). By the same token, the lengthy epilogue of the script (which is of such importance to my present purpose that I shall cite two portions of it at some length) has been in part suppressed entirely in the film version and in part transposed into a single arresting still photograph.

These transpositions and this editing in no way vitiate my contentions concerning the film. But they do stress the desire of the film maker to be absolutely faithful to facts and to practice economy in speculation. Thus what emerges at the end of the film articulates the appalling finality and simultaneously the loose-endedness of modern atheism at its flash point, whereas the script continues to a series of statements which rectify the perspective and emphasize the subjective and transitory quality of the atheism involved, so far as transcending human reality is concerned. There is ample justification for such a shift of emphasis, for this atheism, though transitory from the long-range viewpoint, is a vital and definitive (and defining!) phenomenon of our time.

Script and film alike clearly emphasize the strange ambivalent quality of the Elizabeth Vogler efforts at communication. In both versions, she demonstrably attempts to communicate, and in both versions Alma simply does not grasp the objective fact of the communication, though she is exercised by the suspicion that something has occurred.

Alma obviously is attracted by Elizabeth and specifically by Elizabeth's very hieratic character and persistent silence. This poses a challenge and repeatedly offers to open entirely new horizons to the little nurse, jaded by the very banality of her own "ecstatic" experiences. But at the end Alma simply *will* not respond, *will* not take the difficult path indicated, though in the epilogue, in an access of meticulous fairness, she exonerates Elizabeth of all blame. It is not that Elizabeth has demanded too much; it is quite simply that Alma has not found the courage to abandon her cozy suburban existence, has found herself at the crucial moment unwilling to trade its patient desperation of ordinariness (and security of a sort) for the wild horizons being indicated by this disturbing mask wearer, this omnivorous actress with whom she has sustained a brief and scarring acquaintance. Alma is being asked quite simply to transcend herself, to open up to entirely new horizons, to cast off all security and familiar surroundings and embark on a drastic adventure: that of being *more than herself.* And in some mysterious fashion this involves *at once* the total surrender of her person to that of the Other *and* the resolute willingness to fare forward on her own. Elizabeth as little as Alma wishes any melting of bound-

139

aries of personality; at the supreme moment Elizabeth (in the bedroom visit scene)permits herself a certain maximum of exercise of her serene capacity for transformation; but she *will* not violate the soul of the creature, and thus she withdraws as soon as the creature demands "guarantees" with her petty question about the reality of the conversation in the dark night of love. Alma founders at the end, not because she is doubt-ridden like the knight or glacially aloof like Isak or power-driven like Vogler or neurotically passive like Karin or positively attached to any earthly paradise like Tomas or even openly rebellious like Anna. Alma founders simply because she wants to be herself restrictively and so cannot see the opportunity being offered her (or more accurately *will* not see it) to be herself truly by being more than herself. Man has no meaningful contact with God, said *The Seventh Seal;* man is loveless, said *Wild Strawberries;* out of his lovelessness man makes contact with dark powers, said *The Magician;* the darkest of these powers surge up from man's inmost heart and issue in sterile narcissistic tragedy, said *Through a Glass Darkly;* man must break out of this dark circle and can do so only by some drastic affirmation of God, said *Winter Light;* this affirmation, however, must be free and involve total commitment without any immediate responsive powering, said *The Silence;* therefore, either man must affirm self-transcendence in the terrifying dimension of personal encounter or still definitively the voice of God, says *Persona.*

At the outset of *Persona* things look promising for the sick goddess. If anyone can rally the stubbornly withdrawn, the sick and endangered deity, back to "reality" it is this chattering little product of innocent urban culture and modern medicine. The hieratic stage goddess need not remain dead, need not remain confined in her silent world of unreality, if only she can be made to respond to the ministrations of this fussy, decent little martinet who will bring her truly up to date, wrest her out of the toils of her trenchant transcendence, and warm her thespian coldness with the pleasant earthiness of everyday. Who knows? Perhaps such coldness is the inevitable price of greatness. But it is good for the cold one to be injected with the sunny candor of a nice young nurse. The Incarnation will be undertaken in reverse, by courtesy of man's magnanimity!

Yet Alma herself feels a moment's hesitation at the outset of the experiment. She tells the lady doctor in charge:

> For a moment I thought I ought to resign from the case. . . . Perhaps Fru Vogler ought to have a nurse who is older, who has more experience, more experience of life, I mean. Maybe I can't cope with her. . . . Should Fru Vogler's paralysis be the result of a decision—as it surely must be—after she appears entirely cured . . . then that decision witnesses to a spiritual strength. I believe whoever is to make her really well must have great spiritual strength and power . . .[2]

In the hospital Alma's relationship with Elizabeth has been pretty much confined to medical ministrations; there have been but a few clumsy efforts at homespun psychological rallying of the patient. But when the two travel out to the seaside cottage, when the "retreat" begins and the two are at grips in the absence of the world and all organizational scaffolding, then Alma begins to open up the way to a more personal relationship. She seems to feel that the one way to compel Elizabeth to talk about herself is for the nurse to set the style. But surely this cannot be the only reason impelling Alma to her strange, protracted confession before this beautiful, serene, and sorrowful-faced woman who is her patient. Clearly Alma has felt the magnetism of this enigmatic patient. Elizabeth is never petulant; her steady refusal to speak is neither aggressive nor defiant, merely terrifyingly consistent. And she seems to radiate a kind of serenity that puts Alma entirely at her ease, makes her insensibly shift and interchange the roles of the two of them. Alma's lengthy confession of her sex escapades is distinguished by a disgusting and embarrassing banality rather than by any especially shocking quality. She herself sums up the nauseating silliness of the whole search for meaning and fulfillment within the confines of the exclusively and statically human dimension:

It doesn't make sense, it just doesn't hang together at all, when you begin to think about it. Getting all that upset over trifles. Can you understand what I mean? . . . And what happens to all one's resolutions? Isn't that important at all? Oh, how silly it all is. Well, no reason to start screaming anyway. . . .

I must blow my nose.[3]

But now occurs the first of a series of quietly startling scene events in this climactic film, portrayed with masterly underemphasis by Liv Ullman as Elizabeth:

> *Alma lays her heavy head on the table and pushes her arms out over the edge. She closes her eyes and gasps.*
>
> "Now you must go away to bed, for otherwise you'll go to sleep right here at the table," says Fru Vogler in a low clear voice.
>
> *Alma does not react at once but it gradually dawns on her that Elizabeth is talking to her. She sits up and stares out at the sea. After a wordless interval:*
>
> —Yes, I must go to bed right away. Otherwise I shall certainly go to sleep right here at the table. And that would be really a bit uncomfortable.[4]

In the night visit scene which follows closely upon the brief interchange at the table, every technique of surrealistic camerawork, every nuance of double-exposure photography and simultaneous multidimensional filming, is invoked, to a far greater extent than in any other film of the series, to instill the visual groping after a well-nigh impossible rendezvous:

> *She wakes up: someone is moving in the room. It is a white figure, soundlessly shimmering forth and again retreating toward the door. . . . Slowly Elizabeth approaches, clad in a white nightgown and a little knitted jacket. She comes over to the bed, bends over Alma with infinite caution. Alma seems to be asleep. Then Elizabeth draws back the cover and climbs into Alma's bed, stares a moment at her, draws up her nightgown, and lowers herself gently. The touch is incredibly light, barely perceptible. Elizabeth supports herself with the palm of her hand and bends low over Alma, brushes her cheek with her lips. Her long hair falls over her forehead and hides her face.*

"You can do with me what you will," whispers Alma, "I exist only for your sake." [5]

This moment is the supreme approach to a perfect God-man communication. Man is ready for only a moment, to be sure, but for a supremely vital moment, to accept and adopt the only relational position proper to him or fruitful for him, utterly exposed to the power of God. The crux of the problem is that this act of man has occurred in a transitory half-dream state which man soon takes pains to forget.

Alma will soon reproach Elizabeth bitterly with inability or, worse still, disinclination to understand. But already we have been shown palpably that the difficulty is quite another. First by the softly spoken admonition, then by tactile contact, Elizabeth has been attempting to communicate with this restless girl. Yet Alma herself next morning shows how little she has absorbed; above all she shows how obtuse she is in her waking moments to such communication:

I want to ask you something. Did you speak to me last night?

Elizabeth goes on reading and shakes her head.

Were you in my room last night?

Elizabeth shakes her head again without raising her eyes from her book. Alma leans forward intently over her sewing. [6]

Let a modicum of the naturalistic interpretation stand. Let it be said that Alma's failure to recall exactly what happened that night is due not only to obtuseness but to a disinclination to remember, let it be maintained that there is powerful evidence throughout and especially in that night scene for an interpretation that would stress the human power struggle between the two women, the dreadful clash of wills, the horror assailing Alma that she may somehow be absorbed into the apparently stronger personality, the skittishness of this young nurse at the prospect of being made to surrender herself awhile and then being cast off as her uncommitted lover passes on to another role. All of these undeniably present strands merely reinforce and deepen the theological epiphany. For throughout the entire series of films, man's fears have been Alma's fears; man's muddled and inconstant hope and longing have been Alma's muddled and inconstant, joyful yet timorous, hope and longing. Alma is really neither naturally vicious nor naturally aloof or self-centered; Alma's crucial weakness, *and it is fatal,* is quite simply shallowness and concomitant conceit. Her persistent commitment to the purely human inhibits any deep-thrusting understanding of her patient's affliction or of that patient's real healing power.

This same incapacity to plumb the true depths of the amazing woman who appears to hide behind so many masks is evident in the letter written to Elizabeth by her ineffectual husband, who flits through the increasingly surrealistic closing scenes of the film like a wraith or epiphenomenon:

Dearest Elizabeth,

Since I cannot come to see you, I am writing to you. If you don't want to read my letter, you can leave it be. But I cannot help trying to get through to you. Because I am plagued by a constant anxiety and a constant question: Have I somehow wronged you? Have I somehow hurt you without knowing it? Has some pointless misunderstanding arisen between us? I ask myself a thousand questions and get no answer. As far as I know we were happy just now. Surely we had never been so close. Do you remember how you said: "Only now do I begin to understand what a marriage really involves. You have taught me . . . that we must see one another as two frightened children, full of good will and the best intentions, but at the mercy of powers with which we can only partly cope." [7]

Indeed in the opening scenes there is a haunting counterpoint of implicit accusation and visual refutation revolving precisely around the charge of heartlessness leveled against Elizabeth. For the radio scene in the patient's bedroom clearly implies that Elizabeth herself is wanting in sympathy, that the problem of mutual understanding between her and her husband (and, by extension, between her and Alma) is the fault not of the shallowness and silliness of either of the latter but rather of the stoniness of heart of Elizabeth herself:

> *From the radio is heard a woman's voice:*
>
> Forgive me, forgive me, my darling. You must, you *must* forgive me. Your forgiveness is the one thing I long for. Forgive me and I can go on living.
>
> *The beautiful delivery is interrupted by Fru Vogler's laugh. A warm and hearty laugh. She laughs till the tears come to her eyes. Then she quiets down again to listen. The woman's voice goes on without a break:*
>
> What do you know about mercy? What do you know about a mother's suffering, a woman's tender anguish?
>
> *Fru Vogler breaks out into a laugh as gaily as before. She lifts her arm and takes hold of Alma's hand, draws her over toward the edge of the bed. She fumbles with the radio's volume control. Woman's voice up to more than life-size volume:*
>
> O God, you who are somewhere out there in the darkness that surrounds us all, have mercy on me. You who are love, pure love.[8]

Well may Elizabeth laugh at the posturing pretentiousness of this accusing voice; well may she find bitterly amusing this implication that she herself knows nothing of mercy or the awful anguish of a parent, the anguish compounded of love and amazement at the pettiness and deficiencies of the offspring. The sense of her laughter, of her attack of near hysterics at this bumptious declamation of the unknown voice, is visually explained a few minutes later. When the hospital is still and the conscientious nurse asleep in her little bed, we are shown a brief kaleidoscope of the watching God, alone and exposed to the world's woe, *consequence of the world's stultifying pettiness*:

> *That evening she is watching a TV news summary program. It includes a short of a Buddhist nun burning herself to death on the*

street in protest against the government's religious policy. When Fru Vogler sees this scene, she begins to cry. Her sobs are loud and piercing.[9]

The turning point of the film occurs at the moment when Alma reads Elizabeth's letter to the doctor who has sent her off to recuperate with the sunny young nurse as companion and guardian. For in this letter Alma learns a terrifying truth which she fights desperately to suppress, works diligently to abrogate, strives mightily to overturn: it is quite simply that Elizabeth, though feeling genuine if somewhat amused affection for her, *does not need her at all.*

> *. . . dear Alma . . . spoils me in the most touching way. . . . I believe she is happy and quite attached to me, even a little in love with me in an unconscious and charming way. It is really quite fun to study her. She is quite a chameleon. . . . I encourage her to prattle, it is quite instructive. She moves entirely within the ambit of a conventional religiosity tricked out with her own unaccountable notions. Meanwhile she cries over her past sins (some sort of fleeting orgy with a wild teen-ager and the subsequent abortion). She laments the gap between her principles and her actions. In any case I have her confidence and she tells me all about herself. As you know, I absorb into myself everything I come in contact with: and so long as she doesn't notice anything, it makes no difference . . .*[10]

From this moment, Alma adopts a radically new technique to attain a radically different goal. Previously she had been honestly if mistakenly devoted to the assignment of curing a woman she believed sick. Now she is single-mindedly determined to force that woman to speak, oblivious to the fact that Elizabeth has already spoken "at sundry times and in divers places."

After an unsuccessful attempt to force speech out of Elizabeth by inflicted pain, Alma has recourse to a straightforward and passionate personal appeal, in the course of which for the only time in the film the young nurse appears as an entirely positive and prepossessing or at least disarming person:

> Do you want to do me a great favor? I know it is a sacrifice but just now I need your help.
>
> *Elizabeth looks up from her book. She has caught the intensity of Alma's cadence, and for an instant something enigmatic flickers in her eyes.*
>
> It's nothing dangerous. But I should like you to speak. It needn't be anything noteworthy; for example, we could talk about the weather, or about what we're going to have for dinner, or about whether we think the water's going to get cold after the storm, so cold that a person couldn't go bathing. Can we just chat for a few minutes? Just one single minute? Or you could read something from your book. Or just say a couple of words.[11]

Soon there intervenes the thrust of blasphemy and contumely: "*The thermos flask is standing on the table. Alma opens it and throws the boiling water at Elizabeth.*" [12]

One final thrust is aimed at the heart of the compassionate God as Alma begs forgiveness for all the pain, insult, and even terror she has inflicted on Elizabeth and begs her to grasp or at least try to grasp the fact of Alma's staggering littleness and deficiency:

> Elizabeth, forgive me if you can. I behaved like an idiot. Believe me, I really am here to help you. I don't understand what is happening to me. You see that I am acting like an idiot. You must forgive me. But it was that silly letter.[13]

But finally, depressed and enraged by her continued failure to elicit any response from this beautiful patient, Alma definitively casts in her lot with the New Theologians. She resolves to tell Elizabeth what is really wrong with her. If man cannot compel God to descend to the level of man's own muddled and puling quest for comfort and the easy theological theorem, then God will simply have to be psychoanalyzed out of existence.

Like most modern theologians, Alma seems to imagine she knows not only a great deal of relevant factual material about her subject but, much more important, the key to all the hidden secrets. The nub of Alma's diagnosis is Elizabeth's alleged lust for self-sufficiency and the cold eminence of the stage idol's position. Elizabeth has worn so many masks that she has forgotten or killed her own healthy personality—or maybe she is hiding deliberately behind the masks of the roles she assumes on the stage in order to avoid the terrors of personal confrontation at the level of the flesh. Alma evokes the actress' less than successful marriage and tells her why the marriage has been a failure and its issue condemned to subsist as an unloved child.

At about this point a horrifying new element enters the film: the boundaries of personality between nurse and patient threaten to dissolve entirely. Alma can no longer be sure if she is speaking with her own voice or with that of the persistently silent Elizabeth Vogler. Finally man, who has projected into God the turmoil and deficiency of his own heart, arrives at an absolute crisis of identity and in a frenetic muddled outburst of longing, terror, pity, and revulsion enunciates through Alma's mouth:

> I don't feel like you. I don't think like you. I am not you. I am only supposed to be your nurse. I am Sister Alma. I am not Elizabeth Vogler. You are the one who is Elizabeth Vogler. I will be glad to—I love—I have not—[14]

Now there can be but one denouement, that spine-chilling sequence somewhere out of time, deliberately vaguely backgrounded as befits an absolutely all-embracing symbolic action, like a love act, a Mass, or a crucifixion that is deicide. Suddenly actress and nurse are again in what dimly seems to be a hospital room; against the vague background their two faces stand out with drastic sharpness, the face of God and the face of man on the brink of voluntary atheism, of self-atheization:

> "Try to listen," whispers Alma. "I beg you. Can't you hear what I am saying? Try to answer now."
>
> *Elizabeth lifts her face from her hands. It is naked, sweat-drenched. Then she nods slowly:*
>
> "Nothing, nothing, nothing at all. Nothing."
> "That is good. That's the way it had to be." [15]

Alma is shown immediately after the fade-out of this dreadful sequence, fetching and gaily packing the few belongings she has at the seaside house, running merrily down the road to where a bus is crawling along the highway. She hails it. It stops. Alma is on her way back to the town she loves so well and has missed so much during her enforced retreat in the solitary and secluded place, alone with God.

Elizabeth Vogler has spoken for the first and last time in a voice clearly audible to Alma. God has approved and ratified the proclamation of atheism on the part of his human creature.

The wheel has come full circle. The silence of God that was an austere external challenge is now become an internal reproach. Elizabeth Vogler simply vanishes from the horizon of Nurse Alma, who can now enjoy her urban atheism. But in the narrow room in that morguelike building an alarm clock rings, a boy sits up, blinks uncertainly, and begins tracing with his long mobile fingers on the glass wall. Under the dextrous motion of those young fingers the features of his mother slowly begin to take shape and distinctness, gradually materializing upon the glass.

The beginning of *Persona* is unusual even in the Bergman universe. Initially we see the director's booth in a film reel running through the camera. "Action" is called out of the darkness, and a series of symbols flash on and off the screen, so rapidly as to be almost subliminal: a spider, a hand with a nail being driven through it, a winter forest landscape with patches of watery snow. Clearly this is a hint that the motifs and symbolism of all the preceding relevant films are here being caught up and integrated. At film's end again we see the blank end of the filmstrip running through the camera. The rest is silence.

Thus far the film as presented on the screen. In the Bergman manuscript there is a rather lengthy epilogue which is of supreme importance for our present purpose. The woman doctor is represented as saying:

> In December Elizabeth Vogler went back to her home and her theater. She was warmly welcomed in both. The whole time I was sure she would come back. Her silence was a role like all her

others. After a while she didn't need it any longer and so she laid it aside. It is naturally hard to analyze the innermost motives in a psyche and a spiritual life as complicated as Fru Vogler's.[16]

And Nurse Alma is given two strange and haunting outbursts, one of which was transposed in the filming into a highly arcane though rigidly arresting still photograph, the other being entirely suppressed:

The first Alma utterance is this:

> Day by day I walk my lonely road and keep trying to compose a letter. I know the letter will never be written. Yesterday I stood at your writing table. There I noticed a photograph. It showed a little boy, seven years old, clad in short trousers, ankle socks, and a little fancy overcoat. His face is pale with terror and his black eyes dilated. He holds his hands over his head. Back of him, to one side, men and women . . . stare dumbly at the camera. On the other side stand steel-helmeted soldiers. The one nearest the boy holds his rifle at the ready and the gun is pointed at the boy's back.[17]

The second outburst of Alma is more immediately to our purpose, with its annihilating confession of human ineptitude for the divine:

> I cannot long for another kind of life. In spite of what I've learned from you. I'm so thankful to you, Elizabeth, and you ought never to have any qualms of conscience on my account.[18]

The *Persona* (*prosopon*, mask and reality at once) of Elizabeth Vogler is the theophany of the true God. He has never needed this creature whom he admits to his intimacy; he can admit that creature only on condition that the creature will surrender himself entirely to a radically new dimension, different from any in which he has familiarly moved; God calls that creature gently but firmly and promises him not the comfort of satisfaction but the glory of transformation allied to the continued drama of created freedom. When man falters or recoils from this invitation in all the fullness of its implications, the result can only be that atheism which is simultaneously deicide.

It is no small achievement to turn the fulcrum of modern

atheism through a 180-degree angle, so that what initially seemed a silence indicative of total anterior absence of God from the realm of reality emerges terminally as a silence wrought by man's deicidal hands throttling that God into definitive quiet. Yet it is a supremely bitter achievement in the order of ideals even though it is a supremely accurate diagnosis in the order of the real history of the human condition. Bergman has signally exposed the real roots of modern atheism in man's voluntary rejection of the God who alone could have supplied the medicine for man's mortality. The climactic picture in *Persona*, that radical evocation of the manifesto of modern atheism, that manifesto only Nietzsche had the courage and honesty clearly to articulate and interpret, is absolutely faithful to historical fact.

But it would be exceedingly shallow to suppose that this fidelity of portrayal implies any approval or associational identification. For always as the drama sharpens to its irredeemable climax in the choice of Alma, which is the choice of Satan, ratified for all eternity by God and fixed and unalterable because there is no will to alter it, always in the swirling impetuous dynamic of the fateful action, Bergman presents again and again the tremulous possible option, and each of these evocations is echoed in muted counterpoint in *Persona* itself, even as the symbols of the preceding dramas are evoked at the outset of this final film of the series.

If man cannot die with serene faith, at least he can learn to die crying with Antonius Block: "God, you who are somewhere, who *must* be somewhere, have mercy upon us" [19] (echoed in *Persona* by the radio play voice crying: "O God, you who are somewhere out there in the darkness that surrounds us all, have mercy upon me").

If man cannot break through to openhearted loving, he can at least attain to an incipient realization of his need for love and radical understanding, can learn to cry with Isak Borg: " 'Where is the friend I seek everywhere?' " [20] (echoed in *Persona* in Alma's ingenuous exclamation: "Nobody ever bothered to listen to me. I mean the way you are listening to me now. You are really listening to me. . . . I wanted a sister, always I wanted a sister and all I ever got was a crowd of brothers" [21]).

If man cannot throw off entirely the lust for certainty and power in the human dimension, he can at least gaily venture forth like the lustful but honest young Sara muttering: "Dear, kind people, may I come along? (Pause) I don't know what's happened to me, but I've probably lost my mind. (Pause) It must be the love potion. (Cries) Because I can't think the way I decided I should think" [22] (echoed in far more intense form in Persona in Alma's outburst: "I don't know what is happening to me. You see that I am acting like an idiot . . . ," and above all in Alma's whispered words in the night scene: "You can do with me what you will. . . . I exist only for your sake").

If man cannot find any sure tower of strength within the purely human dimension, it is at least something to have plumbed the depths of that defenselessness like Karin: "Sometimes one is so defenceless. . . . Like children exposed in the desert at night. The owls come flying by and look at you out of their yellow eyes. There are paddings and rustlings and soughings and sighings. And all the damp noses nosing. And wolves' teeth" [23] (echoed in Persona by that phrase from the letter of the poor husband who quotes Elizabeth as saying: ". . . we must see one another as two frightened children, full of good will and the best intentions, but at the mercy of powers with which we can only partly cope").

If man cannot at once come to the realization that the "earthly paradise" is a deceptive frippery romantic dream, it is at least something that he can at times be disturbed as Tomas Eriksson confesses: "We live our simple daily lives. And then some terrible piece of information forces itself into our secure, safe world. It's more than we can bear" [24] (echoed in highly charged fashion in Persona in the scene in which God himself is shocked at the picture of the burning Buddhist nun).

If mankind cannot crush the sullen rebellion of certain members, it is good at least to know that there are Johans left in the world, puzzling over the secret message, human beings to whom God can say of the benighted rebels what Ester says to Johan about Anna: "We love Mummy, you and I" [25] (echoed in *Persona* by Alma's generous efforts to comfort the ineffectual husband of Elizabeth Vogler).

And finally, even in the face of the definitive and free rejection of God, articulated and bodied forth in Alma's awful phrase, there is still the hope fixed forever in the boy who sketches with mobile human fingers the features of his parent on the walls of the morgue for those who lie in darkness and the shadow of death.

Are we left with "the same old God" at the end of this cycle? No and yes. Certainly the main thrust of the series has been a personalization (one might almost say a neuralization) of the entire God-man relationship (highly justified in the light of the hypostatic union!). Certainly the Omega of the series is a disturbingly exposed, disturbingly demanding reality. But, of course, the Alpha is clearly recognizable too as the God who made heaven and earth. Creative evolution applies not to God but to man; however, to man it applies with a vengeance, for God has willed to leave the future and "fate" of the human cosmos in man's hands, so that that "fate" may be transformed into "love" by the creative response of man. This transformation is possible, however, only if man links himself to the ultimate power source; failing this, man can only stumble forward in the shame of his disordered state to the hour not of transfiguration but of the wolf.

OF GOD

The precise syndrome often touted in theist, especially Christian, circles as "modern atheism" is tormentingly present only to the muddled Christian writer with a bad conscience; it is quite foreign to the atheist as such!

Modern atheism is not a mere demand for a more up-to-date God. Christian efforts to answer the cry of the modern atheist in terms of any variant of the strange deities offered by that loosely knit group of speculators designated as Death of God theologians will inevitably fail. If some Christians can live with such a God, modern atheists most certainly cannot. They find him not more convincing but merely revelatory of the extremely curious psychology of their "Christian" interlocutors. The kindly atheist will tend to praise the theistic compromiser for his presumably sincere effort to mythologize what had once been seriously taken as statements of ontological fact. A God who can become man, suffer, die, and rise again is to the modern atheist a mystery beyond comprehension and is rejected as unsupported by sufficient (if any) empirical evidence. But a God who can become man, suffer, die, and never rise again (simply handing on the torch to newly roused man) is to the modern atheist patent nonsense, acceptable only as a mythologized transitional stage to true atheism.

Modern atheism is not a mere insistence on the dignity and inalienable freedom of man. Plenty of convinced theists see no contradiction between a genuine God and free human creatures, though they do see mystery here. And many a modern atheist would sharply disagree with the simplistic Utopian vision of the brave new world of free man: far too many data from the sciences of genetics, parapsychology, psychoanalysis, and geopolitics militate against any clear option in favor of man's untrammeled freedom.

Modern atheism is not a mere critique of institutional religion. Many theists are even crisper in their critique of obsolete and trammeling factors in the human dimension of revealed religion than are the atheists who are persuaded that the whole business is groundless and the institutions therefore already largely irrelevant to modern man—and in any case neither capable of reformation nor worth serious reforming effort.

Modern atheism is a result of inspection of the sum total of reality available to modern man. It enunciates at the end of its inspection: I find nowhere the kind or species of reality designated in the past as God, Allah, Jahweh, or even Supreme Creator. Certainly the atheist will, with pardonable glee, pounce upon all the mysteries of theism as so many unresolved loose ends militating against the cogency of any theistic arguments. But the intelligent, perceptive, and honest atheist in our day will never contend that these mysteries and problems form the true basis of his own atheism: he knows full well that he has mysteries and conundrums enough of his own, and that it is both dishonest and dangerous to contend that unresolved questions invalidate an ontological stance. No, the trenchant modern atheist is basically proclaiming that he simply does not "see" God anywhere.

I would even contend that the real religious turmoil in the twentieth-century human family is almost entirely restricted to the theist camp! It is there that many are scrabbling after a new meaning, a new approach, a new attitude, an "updating" which oscillates between the extremes of a merely prudential modification of outmoded practices to a rearticulation of God himself. It seems at very least not illegitimate to direct the attention of these theists to the possibility that the atheists may be righter than they, that the itching quest after new articulations may be a simple evasion of the massive question: Is God there? Certainly articulations must never be confused with the underlying reality. But here, curiously enough, poetic and aesthetic articulations are tougher and more resistant than theological and philosophical ones. The visceral, the neural, the immediately sensuous experience (positive or negative), can be trusted both to reveal more clearly than any noetic elaboration and to survive longer than any syllogism (whose form may continue impeccable long after its content has evaporated into utter irrelevancy).

At this immediate, neural, visceral level, the old division stands firm: for some, a presence; for others, an absence. But all can more safely and with better hope of some success investigate the data of that immediate experience than they can address themselves to an evolving critique of the intellectual articulations of that radical experience. The intellectual articulation will always be inadequate, and each new improvement will simply replace one inadequacy with another (usually the opposite, as the pendulum swings steadily between the extremes of transcendence and immanence, of unity and plurality, of "grace" and "nature," of predestination and free will). But if we return to the ultimate aesthetic experience, we may find more common ground and likewise more salvific correctives for the intellectual articulation than could ever be supplied within the dimension of that necessarily less immediate operation of intellectual articulation itself.

There is no "new God." There is only the old God more clearly seen, more bravely faced, encountered on man's part with more of the courage displayed by that God himself in creating free creatures. In extremely plastic form, with preeminently plastic images, these films reveal the elements of human experience that lead some to conclude to atheism and others to conclude to theism. It is only essential that the films be approached with a pure heart, i.e., without any *intellectual* prejudices that would exclude from the outset *any* conclusion, however wild, which the facts of experience might seem to indicate. Man has constantly boasted, since the pre-Socratics instituted the philosophical quest, that his great strength is his synthesizing intellect. Perhaps man should consider a moment if the synthesizing effort, needful though it may be, must not constantly be being checked out against the data of primordial experience. It is to that sort of primordial experience that all these films direct our attention.

Yet in one sense this film odyssey may indeed reveal a "new God"; it may highlight the baneful and even blasphemous inadequacy of the time-honored articulations of God in theology. The theologian, I have said, must proceed with care on pain of lapsing into unappetizing heresy. This was not a political but an aesthetic warning. The "heresy" is unappetizing because man's deepest nerves sense that the articulation being offered does violence to some datum of primordial experience. If a sense of freedom, a longing for immortality, a capacity for sacrificial love, is there at the primordial level, no amount of syllogizing at the intellectual level is going to convince man that any of these is insubstantial. If the deep conviction and impression of the essential deadness of the heart of the universe is compellingly present at the aesthetic level, no amount of cunning argumentation at the intellectual level is going to persuade man into a full-throated and heartfelt *credo* at the level of the will.

In many senses this is the "old God," for it is a reality capable of keeping his own counsel, capable of a kind of personal and even mordant relation to seeking man. Gradually the absence lightens into an eerie presence, finally to reveal a Reality utterly exposed to man, voluntarily exposed and deliberately refusing to exercise any omnipotence to prevent deicide if man is determined on that deicide.

In other senses, this is indeed a "new God," for this God has no part whatever in rationalistic formulations, either of restrictive humanism or of mathematicizing transcendentalism. This reality is the One who is appallingly present to man and whom man can somehow kill though man can never grasp entirely the very reality he kills.

The thrust of the film series we have reviewed is the clarification of an initial silence apparently indicative of absence into a terminal silence terribly indicative of presence. What seemed at the outset to be a silence proclaiming God's irrelevance to the human cosmos emerges at the end as a silence proclaiming God's supreme relevance (and even exposure) to human freedom. God is silent not because he is not but because he is *God*, the supreme lover of freedom and thus the supremely silent victim of man's misuse of freedom.

It is entirely false to facts to pose the question of modern atheism in divorce from or even in abstraction from the phenomenon of Christ. Nor, of course, does Bergman do this. With great deftness and sympathy he interweaves the Christ motif into this series of films in most integral fashion, though Christ dominates only one film (*Winter Light*) and appears in the final film in highly symbolic guise, as the boy bringing into focus the features of his parent.

This reticence concerning Christ does not witness to any denigration of his key role *within the Bergman film universe*. It witnesses rather to two historical facts: modern man has demonstrably lost much of his capacity to see Christ as God-made-Man; and the very followers of that Christ have bowdlerized the stunning fact of the Incarnation. Against both these historical mistakes and confusions, Bergman's oblique technique is most powerfully concentrated.

The two errors are more closely connected than might appear at first glance. Bergman's poetic approach allows him to leap the restraining demands of discursive theology to highlight intuitive insights into the drastic existential fact and problematic centering on God's powerful ingress into human history.

Legions of Christians have simply not drawn the ultimate

conclusions from that great fact. Even those who so laudably and validly protest against the mistaken contraceptive Monophysitism that would insulate the divine Logos in a kind of antiseptic space suit within the shadowy human nature so often assumed fail to realize that they can no more isolate the humanity of Christ from the stuff of the material cosmos than they can isolate the divinity of the theandric composite, the God-Man, from his humanity. And if Christ's human nature cannot be insulated from and "purified" of the stuff of the cosmos, then in Christ the entire cosmos, the entire space-time continuum, has in some sense become holy and even deified. From the instant of the Incarnation, the hostile division and contradistinction between the Creator God and the created cosmos has been obliterated. True, this poses frankly for that space-time continuum the same rigorous condition of transfiguration in the dark lands as is posed for man himself. The Incarnation sanctions no restrictive or stagnant earthly paradise, nor does it permit any notion that the kingdom of God can be perfectly and exhaustively realized on this earth. But it does make all things full of the presence of God; and it does forever remove the faintest justification for any setting of the energies of space-time over against the Energy who is God, in sullen or active hostility. The Incarnation does repudiate and abrogate any contention that the material universe must be abandoned in order to find God.

That material universe must indeed be transfigured to the ultimate by man's free collaboration with God, to the ultimate paroxysm whereby material spatiotemporal nature is brought to coil in upon itself for the great dark leap into eternity, where "there shall be no more sea" (Rev. 21:1). But even now, in this our age of torment and terror, the earth is full of the glory of God. And in the age of Christ it is unnecessary and fruitless for the seeker to turn his eyes from the surging powers of the material universe in the hope of more surely contacting a comforting deity in the dimension of eternity. For this God has descended to usward and abides now until time be done in the very fabric of our expanding universe of space-time.

The silence of God weighs heavily throughout the entire film series on precisely those characters who are seeking ultimate logical answers, final and unquestionable certitude. It least troubles those characters who are dedicated to the adventure of freedom (even though they may not know or identify it as such).

The God of Bergman's series is equally dissatisfied with man's decent effort to live a decent moral life and with man's pretentious thrust to a transhuman morality. What this God imperiously demands is perfectly bodied forth in Elizabeth Vogler: a simultaneous total passivity and courageous activity. Neither may man demand of God the perfect geometric answer to all his unsolved problems nor may he presume to impose on God the narrow confines of his human decency and affected morality. Rather must man strive at once to maintain the ridiculous, the well-nigh impossible balance, epitomized in Eric Gill's memorable definition of man's ideal position before God: erect upon his knees! On the one hand accepting entirely his creaturely status, on the other hand valiantly shouldering his moral responsibility, man must fare forward to the good fight, never certain of the outcome, *because he must contribute to that outcome.* The end of the human condition will be no satisfying merely mathematical theorem nor yet (on pain of total chaos) any purely and exclusively human elucubration of happiness or perfection, any merely human "earthly paradise." It will be rather that ideal combination of the impatient and vigorous human thrust to perfection with the divine initiative and condescension. It will be Alma not retreating from her daring night scene confession: "You can do what you want with me. I exist only for your sake"; it will be Johan's openhearted reading of the secret message; it will be Sara's dedication to the adventure of love in improbable surroundings; it will be, at the anterior extreme, at least Antonius Block's despairing but still faithful and believing cry: "God, you who are somewhere, who *must* be somewhere, have mercy upon us."

God is luminously present throughout this entire cycle, but the nature of his presence in each film is substantially conditioned by the state of the human protagonists.

Man is most definitely to be taken seriously as a free created moral being, who by his action or sluggishness in action can really affect the future course of his own and the cosmos' destiny. Will man in fact properly respond? That is the unresolved question: and the mastery, the artistic mastery, of Bergman's staging of the final film of the series, with his drastic suppression of the transcendent element and his equally drastic highlighting of the human element, is proof positive of his absolute artistic integrity. For the outcome is still, in our day, really in the balance. God's reality and power do not change; but man is a chameleon even as Alma was so diagnosed by Elizabeth Vogler. Man can alter his stance and his answer from age to age; and man's answering thrust really matters, desperately matters, is indeed crucial. This is no divine comedy; it is a divine-human tragedy in the sense that it can most definitely have a tragic outcome.

Indeed there is in this context a particularly luminous little scene in *The Silence:*

> ANNA: What are you up to?
> ESTER: Working, as you see.
> ANNA: Then I think you should stick to your work.
> ESTER (*questioning*).
> ANNA: And not spy on me.
> ESTER: Maybe.[1]

In fact God works constantly to effect that salvation that can be finally consummated only by man's free response. Indeed, in the dimension of poetic discourse, God may be reminded of that signal fact that he *cannot* and morally *should not* (in his imperfect human regents and defenders) spy on man's freedom. But Ester's retort on the part of God, within the same dimension of poetic discourse, is not entirely inapposite. Maybe God should stick to his own transcendent salvific work, but woe to man if man imagines that his own human moral response can be perfected in the absence of divine intervention.

The singular contribution of this series to theological interpretation of twentieth-century man lies in its trenchant fidelity to fact, to historical accuracy, and its simultaneous sovereign independence of human particularity. No provincialistic specificity is allowed ever to trammel the generic thrust of the cycle. No question of detail is ever allowed to remain merely a question of detail. Everything, every thought and fear and feeling, is reduced, led back in the strictest metaphysical sense, to the ultimate confrontation between Creator and creature; and the meaning is clear: the gulf can never be bridged by the creature. For he is as powerless as Emanuel Vogler; he can only agitate unquiet preternatural powers unto destruction. Only the Creator can bridge the gulf. But if he resolves to do so, then he too must be ready for a fateful rendezvous. For his extreme of generous exposure may well be met by a human rejection which will produce a transtemporal Calvary. Elizabeth Vogler may stretch forth the arms of her compassion and the power of her arms to a restless Alma and be met with a half-conscious acceptance followed by an entirely conscious repudiation. This is the risk the condescending Creator must take; this is the risk he is resolved to take. He does not whine at the outcome. Only one further point is to be noted, in the context of Bergman's artistic integrity: supposing man, to effect this ultimate rejection of God's advances, opts for radical and terminal atheism, what of God? *His serenity will in no way be affected.* Elizabeth Vogler at the end raises a naked and sweat-drenched face to the rejecting Alma. But God remains true to his own reality and to man's freedom and *ratifies the rejection.*

Man is restlessly active throughout the entire cycle of films: Antonius Block seeks certitude and a redemption from mortality and meaninglessness; Isak Borg seeks refuge from loneliness and terminal mortality and lovelessness inflicted upon him by his personal guilt; Emanuel Vogler seeks power to spring the bounds of humanity and let in even the dark powers he hopes fondly he can control; Karin lusts after the dark thing behind the wallpaper; Tomas Eriksson intends to take Christ's place alone on the cross of doubt and fear; Anna intends to hew out for herself a niche of total independence of the suffocating elder sister; Alma finally throttles God. But God is not inactive either —only his activity is more serene and opaque and mysterious to mortal eyes: Death plays a desperate game with the wandering knight, geared toward transfiguration in the drastic dimension of the dark lands; Isak Borg's old mother cherishes memories of a day when children were properly children even as she fumbles amid the chaos of their growing up; Granny snatches her royal coin from the dark woodland even as her uneasy and restless grandson strives toward a technological mastery of the secrets of the cosmos which he approaches without love; Minus tries to bring the force of God to bear upon a restless human sister; Märta offers the redemptive power of her humanized love to a trenchant seeker after final answers; Ester pours the intolerable light of her presence on a rebellious younger sister; Alma is finally permitted by Elizabeth to strangle God into definitive silence.

God is always active but with profound and *personal* respect for human freedom. Initially this respect is a formal and dignified and unassailable transcendent mastery, deigning to take account of human initiative but building that initiative into his plan. Terminally the scene shifts entirely and a new perspective is offered the viewer upon this erstwhile transcendent God. Now that God is flesh of our flesh and nerve of our nerve, he can truly raise a naked and sweat-drenched face to encounter the final and definitive human rejection.

In this film series God has been brought to life without any infringement of the divine perfection or the divine transcendence. Death in *The Seventh Seal* has a little humor and nothing more; Elizabeth Vogler is a full-blooded human being, but Elizabeth Vogler is as serene ultimately as Death himself even though it is her own death, in the human psychological order, which she accepts and not the death of her human partner.

God prowls the night seeking human response and finding it only in a half-dream state soon forgotten in the busyness of next morning.

The silence of God is a problem at the outset and a tragedy at the end. Initially that silence is a challenge to man and terminally it is the result of man's deliberate rejection. Yet the greatness of God and the precious value of created freedom is nowhere more eloquently witnessed than in Elizabeth Vogler's patient and desperate ratification of Alma's silly and vicious rejection of the divine advance.

At the beginning the God-mouthpiece replies to the impatient questioning: So you know nothing? "I have nothing to tell."

At the end the radiant theophany patiently ratifies the creature's choice: "Nothing, nothing, nothing at all."

For all of this is on the level of logic and theology. Another level persistently intrudes, the level of personal contact, of the rendezvous between the divine and the human, between Creator and fallen creature. This is the rendezvous at the tree. This is the rendezvous at which the creature perfectly asserts his created freedom. God ratifies, and the young hands patiently and persistently pursue the sketching of the face.

Every effort to abstract from the intensely personal encounter of God and human creature is intellectualistic cowardice. For at the heart of the created human universe stands freedom; and freedom is the sign of peril, of unpredictability, and of *choice*.

But the choice, again, cannot be staticized into a harmless repetition of preordained moves or the mere pious performance of a ritual. For the partners are not simple automatons in the thrall of a preordaining mechanistic fate. They are free realities.

Yet, once again, they are radically disparate realities, and it is the mistake of the New Theologians to confound their disparity. Death cannot comfort man in language man would understand; only the visionary Jof can see the good outcome of unflinching yea-saying, even in the face of the supreme and somber visit. The Christ on the moldy, musty crucifix cannot immediately comfort Tomas, because Tomas must be willing to endure more than passively accepted torture; he must be ready to proclaim the holiness of the apparent torturer and to learn that God loves him not as a passive sponge but as an active collaborator, proclaiming the superior glory even as the nails bite into his humanity. Ester cannot translate the message of the transcendent God into the language of the rutting human Anna; she can only leave a secret message for one who has ventured into forbidding hotel corridors. Elizabeth cannot ultimately condescend to Alma's beach level, though she can strain toward an apotheosis of this natural drive to union; and the reason for both facts is quite simply this: God has willed to taste of the terrors of our mortal flesh, but only so that we might become Gods.

There is quite as much staticization abroad in our twentieth century as there is Promethean atheism. Indeed the two threaten to merge into an unholy alliance. Both operating separately are dangerous in the extreme but capable of redemption; conjoined and merged, they are fatal.

Promethean atheism strives to attain for man the status of God, and the result is Albert Vogler or Tomas Eriksson. Staticization strives to bring God down definitively to our human level, and the result is old Isak (with his "friend" ultimately himself) or Alma (with God definitively throttled so that cozy man may continue statically to subsist).

In our age the two threaten to combine, and the result is the horror of Karin or the still grosser horror of Anna. God cannot be possessively, passively absorbed as a panacea nor yet aggressively rejected as a trammeling bond. For we are truly of one blood, we human creatures and he, but the blood is his; and our destiny, if it is to be felicitous, must be a correspondence to the glory of that divine blood. If we seek to make it conform to our parameter, the result can only be sterile incest; if we reject it entirely, in our scrabbling after total independence, the result can only be bestial degradation (as with Anna) or, still worse, definitive atheization (as with Alma).

The dangers of atheization have too long been posed by over-cautious theologians in the function of God's glory; they ought to be posed rather in the function of the bestialization of man. God's transcendent serenity can as little be touched by man's rejection as can Elizabeth's serenity by the rejecting Alma. Elizabeth returns to her home and kindred; it is Alma who walks her lonely way.

A single Scriptural text spans the interval between *The Seventh Seal* and *The Silence*. When the seventh seal of God's reality and purpose is broken, there is silence in heaven for the space of about half an hour. It is the silence of a God determined to respect the freedom of man. And not only "determined" (as by some supervenient Fate) but *personally* willing because of *his* great glory. This creature shall not be dandled or chivied or forced or even reproached; he shall be left entirely suspended in the terrible freedom of a *creative creature*. If he evades, resists, rejects, absconds, throttles, God will ratify the choice. If he faces, submits, accepts, remains, embraces, he will find he is still uncomforted, still unfulfilled, still summoned to wider horizons.

God is at grips with his creature man in a strange night rendezvous which man must not remember clearly, for such a clear remembrance would abort man's sense of his own dramatic responsibility. God in the flesh is hanging on the tree, but the cross must appear a little moldy, lest man misread the sign and imagine that his vocation is simply passive acceptance of redemption and penance for previous defalcation. Man is summoned up onto the tree, even as God came down to the tree. For man is summoned to self-transcendence even as God submitted to radical kenosis.

The mystery of the Incarnation has been radically misread as drastically by millennia of Christians as it was by Tomas Eriksson's flock as they dutifully sang their saccharine closing hymn of the mighty Eucharistic event. Not the leading hand but rather the sweat-drenched face is offered to man, to modern man, with the challenge: Will you go beyond yourself in this sign? As the dubious Caesaropapist emperor claimed to have been told: "In this sign thou shalt conquer," so modern man is faced with the challenge: In this sign thou shalt suffer and, suffering, transform thyself and be transformed, be apotheosized.

Not only dare man not approach God as the answerer of questions and gratifier of human curiosity; man dare just as little approach God as the satisfier of human needs. Rather man must approach God as a free creature approaches his challenging Creator summoning him to a new world indeed. Man must answer.

If the answer is no, then we may expect the earthly paradise, the faintly rotting strawberry beds of Pastor Tomas, so eloquently pilloried by Blom the organist. If the answer is yes, then we may expect the rainswept lowering darkness of Ester's secret message, but also the unpredictable dawn of Elizabeth's imperious summons.

NOTES

1

1. Comment cited on dust jacket of Ingmar Bergman, *A Film Trilogy* (New York: The Orion Press, 1967). To be cited throughout as *T*.
2. *Four Screenplays of Ingmar Bergman* (New York: Simon and Schuster, 1966), to be cited throughout as *FS*, p. xv.
3. *FS*, p. xvii.
4. *FS*, p. xxi.
5. *FS*, p. xxii.
6. *FS*, p. xxii.

2

1. *FS*, pp. 124–25.
2. *FS*, p. 146.
3. *FS*, p. 112.
4. *FS*, p. 148.
5. *FS*, pp. 153–54.
6. *FS*, pp. 155–56.
7. *FS*, pp. 111–13.
8. *FS*, p. 113.
9. *FS*, p. 100.
10. *FS*, p. 163.
11. *FS*, pp. 162–63.
12. *FS*, p. 111.

13. *FS*, pp. 158–59.
14. *FS*, p. 100.
15. *FS*, p. 135.
16. *FS*, pp. 135–36.
17. *FS*, p. 138.

3

1. *FS*, p. 170.
2. *FS*, pp. 169–70.
3. *FS*, p. 173.
4. *FS*, p. 225.
5. *FS*, p. 226.
6. *FS*, p. 226.
7. *FS*, p. 227.
8. *FS*, pp. 216–17.
9. *FS*, pp. 221–22.
10. *FS*, p. 210.
11. *FS*, p. 204.
12. *FS*, p. 207.
13. *FS*, p. 207.
14. *FS*, p. 209.
15. *FS*, p. 208.
16. *FS*, p. 207.
17. *FS*, p. 209.
18. *FS*, p. 232.
19. *FS*, pp. 213–14.
20. *FS*, p. 233.
21. *FS*, p. 232.

4

1. *FS*, p. 249.
2. *FS*, p. 294.
3. *FS*, p. 266.
4. *FS*, pp. 252–53.
5. *FS*, p. 291.
6. *FS*, pp. 248–49.
7. *FS*, p. 269.
8. *FS*, p. 294.
9. *FS*, pp. 250–51.
10. *FS*, p. 246.
11. *FS*, pp. 319–20.
12. *FS*, p. 255.
13. *FS*, p. 276.
14. *FS*, p. 280.
15. *FS*, p. 280.
16. *FS*, p. 281.
17. *FS*, pp. 281–82.
18. *FS*, p. 282.
19. *FS*, p. 286.
20. *FS*, p. 301.

5

1. *T*, p. 45.
2. *T*, p. 38.
3. *T*, pp. 32–33.
4. Cf. *T*, p. 44.
5. *T*, p. 29.
6. *T*, p. 42.
7. *T*, p. 42.
8. *T*, pp. 58–59.
9. *T*, p. 47.
10. *T*, p. 61.
11. *T*, p. 26.
12. *T*, p. 50.
13. *T*, p. 53.
14. *T*, pp. 60–61.
15. *T*, pp. 53–54.
16. *T*, p. 50.
17. *T*, p. 51.
18. *T*, p. 60.
19. *T*, p. 5.

6

1. *T*, p. 104.
2. *T*, p. 98.
3. *T*, pp. 84–85.
4. *T*, p. 87.
5. *T*, p. 87.
6. *T*, p. 85.
7. *T*, p. 101.
8. *T*, p. 93.
9. *T*, p. 104.
10. *T*, p. 104.
11. *T*, p. 73.
12. *T*, p. 86.
13. *T*, pp. 102–3.
14. *T*, pp. 86–87.
15. *T*, p. 70.
16. *T*, pp. 66–68.
17. *T*, pp. 68–70.
18. *T*, p. 69.
19. *T*, p. 68.
20. *T*, p. 91.
21. *T*, pp. 76–77.
22. *T*, p. 80.
23. *T*, p. 81.
24. *T*, p. 85.
25. *T*, p. 82.
26. *T*, p. 95.
27. *T*, p. 94.
28. *T*, p. 94.
29. *T*, pp. 95–96.
30. *T*, p. 78.

7

1. *T*, p. 136.
2. *T*, p. 136.
3. *T*, p. 102.
4. *T*, p. 131.
5. *T*, p. 133.
6. *T*, p. 135.
7. *T*, p. 133.
8. *T*, p. 125.
9. *T*, p. 129.
10. *T*, p. 135–37.
11. *T*, pp. 126–27.

12. *T*, pp. 127–28.
13. *T*, p. 110.
14. *T*, p. 141.
15. *T*, p. 142.
16. *T*, p. 142.
17. *T*, p. 120.
18. *T*, p. 131.
19. *T*, p. 132.
20. *T*, p. 114.
21. *T*, p. 132.
22. *T*, pp. 142–43.
23. *T*, p. 140.

8

1. *Persona*, Kinematografi av Ingmar Bergman, Preface.
2. *Ibid.*, pp. 5–6.
3. *Ibid.*, p. 43.
4. *Ibid.*, pp. 44–45.
5. *Ibid.*, pp. 46–47.
6. *Ibid.*, pp. 47–48.
7. *Ibid.*, pp. 19–20.

8. *Ibid.*, pp. 7–8.
9. *Ibid.*, pp. 21–22.
10. *Ibid.*, pp. 49–50.
11. *Ibid.*, pp. 55–56.
12. *Ibid.*, pp. 59–60.
13. *Ibid.*, p. 63.
14. *Ibid.*, p. 84.
15. *Ibid.*
16. *Ibid.*, p. 85.
17. *Ibid.*, pp. 87–88.
18. *Ibid.*, p. 89.
19. *FS*, p. 162.
20. *FS*, p. 204.
21. *Persona*, pp. 36–37.
22. *FS*, p. 321.
23. *T*, p. 29.
24. *T*, p. 74.
25. *T*, p. 134.

9

1. *T*, pp. 124–25.